S0-AYU-012

# SECRET WARFARE

## Battle Standards Military Paperbacks
## from David & Charles

BATTLE STANDARDS

# SECRET WARFARE

## THE BATTLE OF CODES AND CYPHERS

### BRUCE NORMAN

A DAVID & CHARLES MILITARY BOOK

**British Library Cataloguing in Publication Data**

Norman, Bruce
  Secret warfare: the battles of codes and cyphers.
  1. Espionage. Use of cryptology, to 1985
  I. Title
  327.1'2

  ISBN 0-7153-9456-8

© Bruce Norman 1973, 1989

All rights reserved. No part of this
publication may be reproduced, stored
in a retrieval system, or transmitted,
in any form or by any means, electronic,
mechanical, photocopying, recording or
otherwise, without the prior permission
of David & Charles Publishers plc

First published 1973 in hardback by David & Charles
Publishers plc. This paperback edition published
1989 and printed in Great Britain by
Redwood Burn Limited, Trowbridge, Wiltshire
for David & Charles Publishers plc
Brunel House   Newton Abbot   Devon

Distributed in the United States by
Sterling Publishing Co. Inc,
2, Park Avenue, New York, NY 10016

**Cover photographs**
*Front cover:* Fire Support Base 'Action'. (Aerospace Publishing)
*Back cover:* South Vietnamese soldier giving directions by hand-
signals. (Hulton Picture Library)

# FOR PSYCHE

# Contents

# Contents

# List of Figures

# Acknowledgements

I would like to thank all those who have helped me with this book: the agents and cryptologists to whom I have talked and with whom I have exchanged letters; my colleagues, especially Robin Bootle, who did so much research; Stuart Harris and Harry Cowdy; and most of all, David Khan, whose book *The Codebreakers*, the definitive work on the subject, first aroused my own interest in codes and ciphers.

# Introduction

Codes and ciphers are as old as civilised man. But their extensive use is limited to the last two thousand years—and most of that to the last one hundred. They were used by the Greeks and Romans; by the private secretaries of Lucretia Borgia; by the secret agents of Elizabeth of England. They fascinated Samuel Pepys, who wrote his diary in code. They were studied by Edgar Allan Poe, Sir Arthur Conan Doyle and Ian Fleming, and became an integral part of the mystique of Sherlock Holmes and James Bond.

Codes have killed leaders: Mary Queen of Scots, executed in 1587; Alexander II of Russia, assassinated in 1879; Admiral Yamamoto of Japan, shot down by the Americans in 1943. And codes have influenced the outcome of wars. Had it not been for superior Allied intelligence in World War II, Hitler might have won.

Today there is more interest in codes than ever before. Nations retain huge staffs working on 'intelligence'. The CIA, the KGB, the FBI and MI6. The extent and depth of secret communications is enormous. The American Defense Communications system alone transmits messages at the rate of over 10,000 an hour.

Despite their importance, comparatively little has been written about codes. National security has seen to that. So they remain a mystery, forbidden fruit of which people are a little afraid—figures and numbers which are much too complicated to understand. But in fact the basic principles are simple. Once they are grasped, codes are not difficult and their cold anonymity is brought to life by the warmth of human interest and national drama that surrounds their use. For codes are used by people, by many people, every day: by diplomats, soldiers, spies, crooks, businessmen—by anyone who wants to keep his information secret.

My aim in writing this book is to share some of the excitement and fascination that I had when, three years ago, I stumbled accidentally into the strange world of secret intelligence. I knew nothing of codes—felt I could not possibly understand them. But I travelled the world—New York, London, San Francisco, Paris, Tehran, Rome, Honolulu, Moscow, Hong-Kong. Gradually, codes began to live—became real to me as I spoke to the men and women who were involved in their use: to Hitler's successor, Grand Admiral Karl Doenitz; to Tom Lanphier, the American who killed Yamamoto; to Nadya Gardiner who helped capture the spy Joe K; to the anonymous Japanese in Tokyo who described the mysteries of 'Purple'; and the old woman who asked me to smuggle messages across the Berlin Wall.

The spies and secret intelligence agents in this book are real spies and agents. Their names are their real names and so are the codes they used, except where today's intelligence security decrees that I use a code-name or slightly alter a code. And for anyone who wants to try, the codes can be easily copied. Their use in the past has proved very effective. They can be used as effectively again.

# 1 *The Beginnings*

'Cryptography'—the science of secret writing. From the Greek *kryptos* (secret) and *graphos* (writing); which implies that cryptography is largely a Greek invention. In simple terms, cryptography is the art of sending messages in such a way that the real meaning is hidden from everyone but the sender and the recipient.

There are two ways of doing this—code, and cipher. A code is like a dictionary in which all the words and phrases are replaced by codewords or codenumbers, for example:

| Plain text | Codenumber | Codeword |
|------------|------------|----------|
| a, an | 9213 | HXOF |
| about | 5392 | DAIN |
| about time | 1075 | KJVE |
| Africa | 3698 | OHAB |
| Algiers | 2401 | KPWR |
| armoured car | 4763 | BTYF |
| agree | 7492 | IZGY |

So the secret message: 'Send an armoured car to Algiers' (plain text) may be encoded:

| 8867 | 9213 | 4763 | 5390 | 2401 |
|------|------|------|------|------|

or:

| AMCE | HXOF | BTYF | PQLN | KPWR |
|------|------|------|------|------|

To read a code it is necessary to have a copy of the codebook. Without it, the message seems unintelligible; but with it, encoding and decoding messages is a quick and simple process.

The main difference between a code and a cipher is that a code operates on complete words or phrases and a cipher works on single letters.

There are two basic kinds of cipher—transposition and substitution. In a transposition cipher the letters of the ordinary message, called the plain text, are jumbled to form the cipher text. For example, SECRET (plain text) written in jumbled order RSEETC (cipher text) is a transposition.

In substitution, the plain-text letters can be replaced by other letters, numbers or symbols. For example, in a simple system where the letters of the alphabet are numbered 1 to 26, SECRET will be enciphered 19 5 3 18 5 20. Or the plain-text letters can be replaced by other letters. In a cipher system where a=z and z=a, plain-text SECRET becomes cipher text HVXIVG.

To form a more complex cipher, substitution and transposition are combined. For example, the plain-text SECRET can first be rearranged to form the transposition RSEETC. Then on the letters of this transposition, work the above number substitution to make 18 19 5 5 20 3 or, with the above letter substitution, I H V V G X. The word 'secret' has now been enciphered twice, a transposition and a substitution, and will therefore be more secure than if it had been enciphered only once.

The important thing is to disguise the message in such a way that someone who has the code or knows the cipher can understand it whereas someone who does not know the secret, cannot. It is the struggle to break the code or cipher *without* knowing the secret that has exercised men's minds for two thousand years and which adds so much to the drama and excitement of cryptography.

One of the first generals to use cipher was Lysander of Sparta in 405 BC. Lysander was the most powerful man in the Greek world—but the Persians who had supported him in his fight against Athens were envious. He could no longer be sure of their intentions. What should he do? Should he attack Persia and risk losing a valuable ally or should he wait— and risk being surprised and defeated by them? One wrong move and both he and Sparta would be lost. It was a difficult situation crying out for secret intelligence to reveal the real intentions of the Persian king.

As Lysander pondered what to do, a slave arrived with a message. Lysander read it, asked for the slave's belt and then dismissed him. The letter was a blind; it was the belt that Lysander was waiting for. Written along the length of the belt was a meaningless jumble of letters. Lysander took out his *skytale*, a cylindrical baton, something like a policeman's truncheon, and wound the slave's belt spirally round it. As he did so, the meaningless letters were transposed and brought into a new association with one another to spell out a message.

The Persians were false, had murdered Lysander's friends and were scheming against the general himself. It was the vital information Lysander needed. He acted at once, sailing against the Persians and to ultimate victory.

This first recorded use of a transposition cipher saved a general, and saved an empire. It paved the way for the overthrow of the East by the West and the establishment of our own civilisation—a civilisation in which the use of code and cipher was to play an important part.

One of the first generals to use a substitution cipher was Julius Caesar, who invented his own. He would take a message and move each letter of the plain text three places down the alphabet. Thus CHARGE would become FKDUJH. Or the Latin 'Habes opinionis meae testimonium', which Caesar wrote to

Cicero, would be enciphered (using the modern alphabet):

    KDEHV    RSLQLRQLV    PHDH    WHVWLPRQLXP.

It is so simple as to offer no security whatever to code-users of today. But in 60 BC, before cryptanalysis, the science of solving ciphers, had been invented, it was sufficient to keep correspondence secret from unauthorised eyes. And, even to this day, a 'Caesar alphabet' is the name given to any cipher alphabet that is constructed on the same principle as the Roman original.

A more complex version of the substitution cipher was a Greek invention. It arranges the alphabet in the form of a square, and substitutes figures for letters. Numbered from one to five horizontally, and one to five vertically, twenty-five squares are filled by the letters of the alphabet, either in normal order, or, to make things more difficult, in jumbled order, as in Fig. 1. As there are only twenty-five squares for twenty-six letters, one square has to do double duty. Almost always it is I and J that double up.

|   | 1 | 2 | 3 | 4 | 5 |
|---|---|---|---|---|---|
| 1 | L | B | O | S | F |
| 2 | E | V | U | G | R |
| 3 | X | A | M | C | Y |
| 4 | N | T | D | Z | K |
| 5 | W | H | I/J | Q | P |

Fig. 1

A message is enciphered by reading off the letters' number equivalents—first the number down the side and then the number across the top. So the number for A is 3, from the side column, and 2, from the top column, written: 32. In this way the message CHARGE becomes 34 52 32 25 24 21.

One of the disadvantages of writing messages in this way is that the spaces between the numbers are the same as the spaces between the original letters. This immediately tells anyone who is trying to crack the message how many letters or words he is dealing with. To confuse the codebreaker, code messages are therefore usually written in five-figure groups, called code groups. So the above message would today be written 34523 22524 21000. The last three noughts are not part of the message and are called nulls. They are put there to complete the five-figure group and confuse the codebreaker, who will not be able to tell where the message really ends. The use of nulls was a refinement unknown to the Greeks, but their squared alphabet idea was to be of enormous importance two thousand years later in World War I (see p 64).

# 2    *The Renaissance*

The fall of the Roman Empire was accompanied by the eclipse
of cryptography. It was only to reappear a thousand years
later in Italy in the sixteenth century. This was a time of tur-
moil and intrigue, when families like the Borgia and the Medici
struggled for financial and political power. In the climate
created by cloak-and-dagger politics, codes offered a new kind
of security and political advantage.

These codes were as embryonic as the emerging civilisation
that produced them. They were based, like the rest of Renaissance art and ideas, on Greek and Roman precedents. But soon
there were innovations, and the major innovators were mostly
learned men in touch with the political in-fighting of church
and state.

Abbot Trithemius was a Benedictine monk who lived in
Germany. In 1518 he published the first book on cryptography.
It was called *Polygraphia* and was printed in Latin. Soon afterwards it was reprinted in French and German—indicative of
the interest it aroused and the need that it supplied.

Trithemius' encipherment system is a classic of its kind, and
its basic idea has been much copied down the centuries. It is
yet another simple substitution cipher—but with a difference.
Instead of using letters or signs, each letter of the plain text
is replaced by a word or phrase, so that the enciphered word
will read like an ordinary sentence, and so conceal the exis-

tence of a cipher. For example, the first four letters of the Abbot's alphabet read:

| A | B | C | D |
|---|---|---|---|
| I hail thee | beautiful | lovely | we hasten |
| Mary | Pallas | Isis | Astarte |
| filled | magnified | devoted | enthroned |
| of grace | of enticement | of knowledge | of charm |
| the Lord | a god | desire | felicity |
| with thee | at thy breast | in thy arms | in thy heart |
| thou art blest | thou art admired | thou art the shield | loved |
| of women | of the miserable | of all wise men | of lovers |
| fruit | work | delicacy | treasure |
| is blest | is eternal | is admirable | is adorable |

There are several words or phrases for each letter, and any one of them can be used as a substitute for a letter in a message. Thus, the word BAD can be enciphered 'Beautiful Mary is adorable' or 'Pallas is blest in thy heart' or 'A god, I hail thee, Astarte'. The choice is considerable. So with CAB: 'Lovely Mary thou art admired'; 'of all wise men, the Lord is eternal'; 'Desire filled at thy breast'. Not content with one alphabet like this, Abbot Trithemius concocted fourteen and the sender of a message could choose his phrases from any one of them— though, to avoid confusion, it was necessary for him to state at the outset which alphabet he was using.

Trithemius' invention is more important historically and theoretically than practically. It showed how it was possible in a letter to conceal absolutely the existence of a secret message. It showed how a message in one language, say Latin, could be encoded in another, say English, as the encipherment works on the alphabet that is common to them both. It showed, too, how to make a cipher secure. Because of the vast number of alternative words and phrases, codebreakers would have to accumulate an enormous amount of intercepted material before they could find a sufficient number of repetitions to enable them to break the cipher (see pp 43–5, below).

But the serious practical difficulty of Trithemius' cipher is that it makes a message up to fifteen times as long as the original; anyone in a hurry to communicate secret information could not have used it. And, after all, the purpose of code is to transmit information not only securely but quickly.

Trithemius' work was considered by some who read it as closely akin to black magic. All available copies of the book were publicly burnt and the abbot was fortunate not to be burnt with them.

In 1556, Girolamo Cardano, a Milanese doctor and mathematician, published a revolutionary cipher system that still bears his name—the Cardano grill. At its most simple it is a piece of paper or stiff card with a series of holes cut in it. The holes are numbered in haphazard order and correspond to the number of letters in the secret message. To send a message, the grill is placed over a piece of paper and the letters of the message are written through the windows of the grill in the order in which the windows are numbered. This produces, on the paper underneath, a meaningless jumble of letters, which can be further concealed by constructing an innocuous message around them. The recipient deciphers the message merely by placing an identical grill over the text and reading the letters revealed through the windows. For example, consider the innocent-seeming message: 'It is impossible for Paul to come on Wednesday but maybe you could manage a Friday?' (Fig. 2). The specially prepared grill is placed over the sentence and through the windows are revealed the letters of the secret message (Fig. 3). These jumbled letters, read in the order in which the windows are numbered, give the message SEND SUPPLIES.

For short messages the method is quite effective. For longer

IT IS IMPOSSIBLE
FOR PAUL TO COME
ON WEDNESDAY BUT
MAYBE YOU COULD
MANAGE A FRIDAY?

Fig. 2

Fig. 3

| | | | | | |
|---|---|---|---|---|---|
| | 8 | | 1 | | 5 |
| 3 | | | | 9 | |
| | | | | | |
| 6 | | | 2 | | |
| | | 4 | 7 | | |
| | | | | | |

Fig. 4

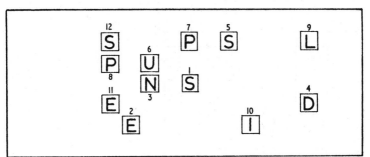

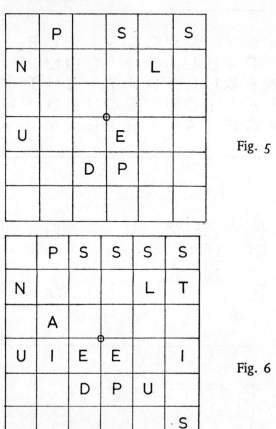

Fig. 5

Fig. 6

ones, Cardano invented a more ingenious device: a grill divided into thirty-six squares, pivoted in the middle. Nine of the thirty-six squares are punched out and numbered (Fig. 4). As in the previous method, the secret message is written through these numbered windows. The message is: SEND SUPPLIES AS SITUATION DESPERATE. The grill is placed over the paper and the first nine letters of the message written

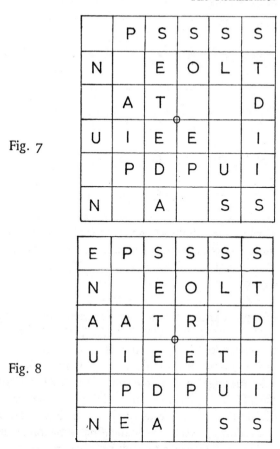

Fig. 7

Fig. 8

in numbered order (Fig. 5). The grill is now rotated clockwise on the central pivot through a quarter-turn, and the next nine letters written (Fig. 6). Another quarter-turn and another nine letters. Gradually the square builds up—the holes in the grill so constructed that two letters never fall in the same place (Fig. 7). Finally, the last turn and the last letters of the message (Fig. 8). This leaves four squares unfilled. These are dangerous

23

| | | | | | |
|---|---|---|---|---|---|
| E | P | S | S | S | S |
| N | E | E | O | L | T |
| A | A | T | R | I | D |
| U | I | E | E | T | I |
| S | P | D | P | U | I |
| N | E | A | S | S | S |

Fig. 9

as they might help an enemy to solve the cipher system, so the square is completed with nulls. In this case it is best to use letters that are similar to those already in use—E, S and I (Fig. 9).

For transmission the message is rearranged in six-letter groups, starting at the top left hand of the square, to give EPSSSS NEEOLT AATRID UIEETI SPDPUI NEASSS. To read the message, the recipient reassembles the letters in the square and then rotates an identical grill in a clockwise direction. The message will come out: SENDSUPPLIESASSITUATION DESPERATESISE. It is not difficult to see where the word divisions come and that the last four letters are nulls.

Cardano's system was the first appearance in the modern world of a transposition cipher. It survived to form the basis of one of the most successful British naval ciphers of World War II.

The title 'Father of Modern Cryptography' is disputed by two men, an Italian called Giovanni Battista Porta, and a Frenchman called Blaise de Vigenère. In 1565, Porta, a Neapolitan mathematician, published a system of substitution ciphering that enabled any one letter of the plain-text message to be written in any one of eleven different ways. Adjusted to the modern alphabet, which gives thirteen different ways of encipherment, Porta's encipherment table is shown in Fig. 10.

| AB | A | B | C | D | E | F | G | H | I | J | K | L | M |
|----|---|---|---|---|---|---|---|---|---|---|---|---|---|
|    | N | O | P | Q | R | S | T | U | V | W | X | Y | Z |

| CD | A | B | C | D | E | F | G | H | I | J | K | L | M |
|----|---|---|---|---|---|---|---|---|---|---|---|---|---|
|    | O | P | Q | R | S | T | U | V | W | X | Y | Z | N |

| EF | A | B | C | D | E | F | G | H | I | J | K | L | M |
|----|---|---|---|---|---|---|---|---|---|---|---|---|---|
|    | P | Q | R | S | T | U | V | W | X | Y | Z | N | O |

| GH | A | B | C | D | E | F | G | H | I | J | K | L | M |
|----|---|---|---|---|---|---|---|---|---|---|---|---|---|
|    | Q | R | S | T | U | V | W | X | Y | Z | N | O | P |

| IJ | A | B | C | D | E | F | G | H | I | J | K | L | M |
|----|---|---|---|---|---|---|---|---|---|---|---|---|---|
|    | R | S | T | U | V | W | X | Y | Z | N | O | P | Q |

| KL | A | B | C | D | E | F | G | H | I | J | K | L | M |
|----|---|---|---|---|---|---|---|---|---|---|---|---|---|
|    | S | T | U | V | W | X | Y | Z | N | O | P | Q | R |

| MN | A | B | C | D | E | F | G | H | I | J | K | L | M |
|----|---|---|---|---|---|---|---|---|---|---|---|---|---|
|    | T | U | V | W | X | Y | Z | N | O | P | Q | R | S |

| OP | A | B | C | D | E | F | G | H | I | J | K | L | M |
|----|---|---|---|---|---|---|---|---|---|---|---|---|---|
|    | U | V | W | X | Y | Z | N | O | P | Q | R | S | T |

| QR | A | B | C | D | E | F | G | H | I | J | K | L | M |
|----|---|---|---|---|---|---|---|---|---|---|---|---|---|
|    | V | W | X | Y | Z | N | O | P | Q | R | S | T | U |

| ST | A | B | C | D | E | F | G | H | I | J | K | L | M |
|----|---|---|---|---|---|---|---|---|---|---|---|---|---|
|    | W | X | Y | Z | N | O | P | Q | R | S | T | U | V |

| UV | A | B | C | D | E | F | G | H | I | J | K | L | M |
|----|---|---|---|---|---|---|---|---|---|---|---|---|---|
|    | X | Y | Z | N | O | P | Q | R | S | T | U | V | W |

| WX | A | B | C | D | E | F | G | H | I | J | K | L | M |
|----|---|---|---|---|---|---|---|---|---|---|---|---|---|
|    | Y | Z | N | O | P | Q | R | S | T | U | V | W | X |

| YZ | A | B | C | D | E | F | G | H | I | J | K | L | M |
|----|---|---|---|---|---|---|---|---|---|---|---|---|---|
|    | Z | N | O | P | Q | R | S | T | U | V | W | X | Y |

Fig. 10

There are thirteen cipher alphabets, each one governed by two key-letters—seen in the left hand column. A key-letter is one that is deliberately chosen to determine the way in which the cipher alphabet will operate. If the key-letter in use is either A or B, then the first alphabet is the one used and, for example, HIDE is enciphered UVQR. The first thirteen letters of the alphabet are replaced by the second thirteen, and vice versa. If the key-letter in use is K or L, then the sixth alphabet is used and HIDE is enciphered ZNVW.

The whole Porta system operates through the use of key-words—any word you like, though shorter ones are easier to remember. Take, for example, the key-word WEST and the message SEND REINFORCEMENTS. Above the message the key-word is written over and over again.

```
Key-word:   W E S T   W E S T W E S T W E S T W E
Plain text: S E N D   R E I N F O R C E M E N T S
```

The key-letter W over the plain-text letter S means that S will be enciphered by the WX alphabet in the cipher table. The key-letter E over the plain-text letter E means that the plain-text E will be enciphered by the EF alphabet in the table. And so on, to give:

```
Key-word:   W E S T   W E S T W E S T W E S T W E
Plain text: S E N D   R E I N F O R C E M E N T S
Cipher text: H T E Z   G T R E Q M I Y P O N E I D
```

A different key-word, such as INFANTRY, gives a completely different encipherment, even though the cipher tables remain exactly the same:

```
Key word:   I N F A   N T R Y I N F A N T R Y I N
Plain text: S E N D   R E I N F O R C E M E N T S
Cipher text: B X L Q   L N Q B W I C P L V Z B C M
```

The variations are as numerous as the number of suitable key-words, so the great strength of the system is that repetitions are infrequent. In the second example the E's in the plain-text message are enciphered in four different ways—X N L Z. It is this that keeps the cipher secure, because it is repetition, as we shall see later, that leads to codebreaks.

Porta's system was a great advance but, though it was secure, it had disadvantages. Because of the complex arrangement of alphabets, both the sender and the receiver would have to carry the cipher tables about with them. This immediately exposes them to the danger of detection. The cipher can be stolen, and the carrier executed for spying. This problem was overcome by Blaise de Vigenère. Born in 1523, he studied at the French court, entered the diplomatic service and travelled widely in Europe. Whilst in Rome he was introduced to cryptography and read Trithemius and Cardano as well as Porta. He published his own work *Traicte des Chiffres* in 1585. Like Porta's, Vigenère's cipher method is based on a table. Its great advantage is its simplicity. Messages can be enciphered easily and quickly; and it is secure—the whole system can be carried in the head.

The Vigenère table is a simple square, twenty-six letters by twenty-six. Along the top are written the key-letters and down the side the plain-text letters (Fig. 11). As with Porta's system, it operates on key-words. Any word is acceptable as long as it contains no letter twice. For example, EAST, and the message to be enciphered, SEND HELP AT ONCE.

Key-word:  E A S T   E A S T   E A   S T E A
Plain text:  S E N D   H E L P   A T   O N C E

Our first plain-text letter S is to be enciphered with the alphabet controlled by the key-letter E. On the Vigenère table take a line from the key-letter E at the top of the table and another

## KEY LETTERS

|   |   | A B C D E F G H I J K L M N O P Q R S T U V W X Y Z |
|---|---|---|
|   | A | a b c d e f g h i j k l m n o p q r s t u v w x y z |
|   | B | b c d e f g h i j k l m n o p q r s t u v w x y z a |
|   | C | c d e f g h i j k l m n o p q r s t u v w x y z a b |
|   | D | d e f g h i j k l m n o p q r s t u v w x y z a b c |
|   | E | e f g h i j k l m n o p q r s t u v w x y z a b c d |
|   | F | f g h i j k l m n o p q r s t u v w x y z a b c d e |
| P | G | g h i j k l m n o p q r s t u v w x y z a b c d e f |
| L | H | h i j k l m n o p q r s t u v w x y z a b c d e f g |
| A | I | i j k l m n o p q r s t u v w x y z a b c d e f g h |
| I | J | j k l m n o p q r s t u v w x y z a b c d e f g h i |
| N | K | k l m n o p q r s t u v w x y z a b c d e f g h i j |
|   | L | l m n o p q r s t u v w x y z a b c d e f g h i j k |
| T | M | m n o p q r s t u v w x y z a b c d e f g h i j k l |
| E | N | n o p q r s t u v w x y z a b c d e f g h i j k l m |
| X | O | o p q r s t u v w x y z a b c d e f g h i j k l m n |
| T | P | p q r s t u v w x y z a b c d e f g h i j k l m n o |
|   | Q | q r s t u v w x y z a b c d e f g h i j k l m n o p |
| L | R | r s t u v w x y z a b c d e f g h i j k l m n o p q |
| E | S | s t u v w x y z a b c d e f g h i j k l m n o p q r |
| T | T | t u v w x y z a b c d e f g h i j k l m n o p q r s |
| T | U | u v w x y z a b c d e f g h i j k l m n o p q r s t |
| E | V | v w x y z a b c d e f g h i j k l m n o p q r s t u |
| R | W | w x y z a b c d e f g h i j k l m n o p q r s t u v |
| S | X | x y z a b c d e f g h i j k l m n o p q r s t u v w |
|   | Y | y z a b c d e f g h i j k l m n o p q r s t u v w x |
|   | Z | z a b c d e f g h i j k l m n o p q r s t u v w x y |

Fig. 11

line from the plain-text letter S at the side of the table and
where they cross is the encipherment letter—W. Repeat the
process with the second letters—key-letter A, plain-text letter
E, and where they cross is E. The completed encipherment
reads: WEFW LEDI ET GGGE.

The strength of the system is shown in how three of the
four letters of the last word all produce the same confusing
cipher letter G, and how also, quite by chance, all letters E in

the plain text also produce E in the cipher text. In some instances this could be dangerous, but as plain-text A of 'AT' also produces an E, the situation is made more confusing for any potential codebreaker. To decipher messages, the system is operated in reverse.

Vigenère claimed that his cipher was unbreakable. It was not, but most people thought it was, and it remained intact for almost two hundred years.

To understand the workings of any of these Renaissance ciphers—Trithemius, Cardano, Porta and, particularly, Vigenère—is to understand the fundamental principles of all encipherment work. It is largely on the work of Vigenère that all subsequent ciphers have been based.

# 3    *Elizabethan England*

The English came late to the Renaissance and late to cryptography. They produced no great theorists like the Italians and French, but they did produce one of the world's outstanding practitioners. Francis Walsingham, head of Queen Elizabeth's secret service, devised methods of operating an intelligence network that were the precursors of British intelligence methods used to this day.

Walsingham, in 1565, in the earliest years of Elizabeth's reign, was a young man recently returned from Italy. He brought with him several manuals of cryptography, including the book by Cardano. From that date, Walsingham was to devote his life to the protection of his sovereign. England, Protestant and with few foreign friends, was beset by Catholic enemies. Walsingham saw at once that the major threat would come from Philip II, King of Spain. Philip had been the husband of England's previous monarch, Elizabeth's Catholic sister, Mary Tudor. It was Philip's ambition to make England Catholic again, and if Elizabeth would not turn Catholic voluntarily then the Catholic Mary Queen of Scots must be put in Elizabeth's place.

London swarmed with enemy agents, and in 1571 Walsingham was given government money to set up Britain's first counter-intelligence network. It immediately produced results and Walsingham revealed to a startled and partly disbelieving

Elizabeth that the recently discovered Ridolfi plot to assassinate her and put Mary on the throne, was, in fact, sponsored by her brother-in-law, Philip of Spain himself. Counter-intelligence, as Walsingham knew, was essentially a defensive operation. To keep more than one jump ahead of Spain he needed to go onto the attack. The English secret service began to operate abroad. Tentacles reached into the very hearts of the intelligence bureaux of Catholic Europe with English agents planted under the very nose of Philip of Spain and even of the Pope himself. Walsingham was so efficient that information sent from Rome was known in London even before it reached Spain. Today, with modern means of communication, that is not such a remarkable feat—but then, with communication restricted to enciphered letters carried by messenger on horseback, it was unheard-of.

To keep his network running smoothly, Walsingham established a spy-school. He used his own London house and when government funds proved inadequate, his own money, as the penny-pinching Elizabeth, on whose behalf all the effort was expended, was too mean to use her own. His school taught cipher and forgery and gave potential agents a thorough grounding in field-work. The most proficient graduate of the cipher school was Thomas Phelippes, soon to become Walsingham's assistant, and England's first great cryptanalyst. The most famous secret agent graduate was Christopher Marlowe, the dramatist, who later died in a tavern brawl in south London. Or was it an assumed death arranged by Walsingham to enable Marlowe to operate more freely? Walsingham knew that a man who is officially dead starts, as an agent, with an enormous advantage over his more obviously alive rivals. Another young man who took Walsingham's course was a Catholic called Gilbert Gifford. Gifford was in trouble with the authorities and, to save his neck, offered to spy on his fellow Catholics. He was an ideal recruit. He loved intrigue, had little conscience, and, because Walsingham had a hold over him, was bound to do as he was told. Walsingham had great plans for Gifford.

Mary Queen of Scots, ousted as queen by her own Scottish subjects, had thrown herself on her cousin Elizabeth, for protection. Elizabeth had replied by placing this dangerous heir to the throne of England in semi-captivity. Many of Mary's co-religionists regarded her as the rightful queen, and Walsingham, with the Ridolfi plot still in mind, knew that Mary was not averse to giving encouragement to the men who schemed on her behalf.

Walsingham was determined to get rid of Mary, and Gifford would be the means. Gifford was installed in a country house close by the one occupied by Mary. It was not long before Mary's people heard of the good young Catholic gentleman who, it was said, secretly professed undying loyalty to the Catholic queen. Mary summoned him. She was convinced of his sincerity and suggested he should become her messenger. Gifford, on one knee and kissing her hand, swore that he was prepared to die for her and his religion. Thus Gifford became, if not the first double-agent, certainly one of the more treacherous.

Gifford devised a method of smuggling letters to the queen in the beer barrels that were regularly delivered to her household. They were brought out in the same way so that Mary, largely out of touch with the outside world before Gifford's arrival, now had a perfect means of two-way communication with her supporters. Mary's correspondence was always enciphered. She never revealed the cipher to Gifford—but, once he had the letter from the beer barrel, he opened it, copied the enciphered contents, sealed it so cleverly that no one could have known it had been opened, and delivered the letters in the usual way. The copies, however, were sent to London where they were deciphered by Thomas Phelippes. Mary was using a simple substitution cipher plus inserted code signs.

Once the code had been broken, subsequent messages, even when the cipher key was changed, provided no security.

As the plots to put Mary on the throne thickened, so Walsingham's noose was drawn tighter. Anthony Babington, the most recent young Catholic gentleman to fall under Mary's spell, had already secured numerous assurances from fellow Catholics that, if there was a sudden vacancy of the English throne, they would rise in support of Mary's cause. Philip of Spain would supply an army and all that was needed was Mary's co-operation.

The first letter Gifford provided for Walsingham revealed Babington's full-scale plot to assassinate both Elizabeth and Walsingham himself. Six young men of Elizabeth's own household were in the scheme and Babington gave their names. But he gave them in code numbers and there was no way for Walsingham to discover their identity. Before he could act, Walsingham needed two things—proof of Mary's support and the identities of the men concerned. He waited. Gifford continued to intercept messages and, within a month, Mary condemned herself when she suggested improvements in Babington's scheme. But still Walsingham waited. He could afford to. Babington, to get Spain's active help, needed to go in person to the Spanish Netherlands. He needed a passport and the man who ran the passport office was, of course, Walsingham.

Babington applied for the passport direct to Walsingham himself. Walsingham was not at home and, whilst Babington waited, a note was delivered to the office ordering a watch to be kept on him day and night. Babington, as Walsingham intended, caught a glimpse of the note, read it and ran. A watch was put on every ship in every port in England and the hue and cry for Babington flushed the six unknown men from cover. Within days, they were all caught; within weeks Mary was on trial for her life.

As well as the evidence supplied by the intercepted letters, the most damaging evidence at this trial were fifty cipher keys, the entire equipment of the papal ciphering bureau, discovered in her apartment. Mary claimed that the letters were Walsingham's forgeries and the ciphers deliberately planted. This is unlikely, but Walsingham, like all great spy-masters, kept few records, so it is not known for certain whether Walsingham or Mary was telling the truth. But the object of Walsingham's exercise was to get a conviction. And he got it. On 8 February 1587, in the great hall of Fotheringay Castle, Mary Queen of Scots was beheaded—one of the first and most distinguished victims of England's cryptographic know-how.

In England, in the century that followed, head-losing amounted almost to a natural consequence of using poor ciphers. Much of Parliament's case against Charles I was based on the contents of Charles' deciphered private letters. Charles was executed in 1649. So, later, were his natural grandson, the Duke of Monmouth, and his friend the Duke of Argyll, in 1685. Monmouth's plan to rebel and seize the throne was conveyed in one of Argyll's letters intercepted by the agents of the new king, James II. The letters were deciphered, the rebellion revealed and the new king's throne preserved, at least for a while, by his cryptographer.

One man who kept his head was Charles II. There may, of course, be no direct connection, but he is known to have used good ciphers.

# 4 The Race for Security

The next great developments in cryptography came in the nineteenth century, as the nations of Europe built empires and struggled for world supremacy. In a hundred years, it grew into the science that we know today.

Simple code security was now fairly easy to achieve. What was lacking was speed of transmission. Messages still had to be sent on horseback until, in Napoleon's France, M. Chappe invented the 'lightning telegraph'. This consisted of a series of poles with attached arms, distributed across the breadth of France, each in sight of the other and manned by an operator. The position of the arms carried the news of military victory or defeat, or any other simple message that needed to be conveyed at maximum speed. In this way, news from Strasbourg could reach Paris twelve hours faster than ever before.

The system was primitive. It was not at all secure, as anyone with a little intelligence could guess what the position of the arms meant. But, for all that, it was a major breakthrough. The idea was developed in 1817 by an English naval officer, Captain Frederick Marryat. He used coloured flags and called it semaphore. In 1832, the American S. F. B. Morse invented his electromagnetic telegraph and, by 1838, his alphabetic system of signals to go with it. Morse code is not really a code at all but a substitution cipher with dots and dashes replacing letters:

| | | | | | | | |
|---|---|---|---|---|---|---|---|
| A | ·— | J | ·——— | S | ··· | 2 | ··——— |
| B | —··· | K | —·— | T | — | 3 | ···—— |
| C | —·—· | L | ·—·· | U | ··— | 4 | ····— |
| D | —·· | M | —— | V | ···— | 5 | ····· |
| E | · | N | —· | W | ·—— | 6 | —···· |
| F | ··—· | O | ——— | X | —··— | 7 | ——··· |
| G | ——· | P | ·——· | Y | —·—— | 8 | ———·· |
| H | ···· | Q | ——·— | Z | ——·· | 9 | ————· |
| I | ·· | R | ·—· | 1 | ·———— | 0 | ————— |

The importance of morse was enormous. For the first time, messages could be sent at great speed in almost any language, as the system operated for all languages that used the Roman alphabet.

In 1866, the first telegraph cable was laid across the bed of the Atlantic, and nations could now keep in touch within seconds. The new speed of transmission meant that military, diplomatic or commercial manoeuvres could be directed from a home base thousands of miles from the action. It also meant that as the cables were public and the morse code simple, anyone could listen in and understand the messages. Ciphers now became obligatory if communications were to be kept secret.

Cryptography received a further boost in the 1860s from the American Civil War which emphasised once again the great advantage of using codes and ciphers in a wartime situation. A fairly simple word transposition cipher, with a few codewords thrown in, was sufficient for the Union side to baffle the Confederates. A typical message read:

To George C. Maynard, Washington:
Regulars ordered of my to public out suspending received 1862 spoiled thirty I dispatch command of continue of best otherwise worst Arabia my command discharge duty of my last for Lincoln September period your from sense shall duties the until Seward ability to the I a removal evening Adam herald tribune.

Philip Brunner

The address and signature were cover-names and not part of the message. The first word, 'Regulars', was a codeword that indicated how the message should be written out—in five columns of nine words each—in order to be comprehensible. Following the instructions, it looked like this:

| *tribune* | Lincoln | *spoiled* | | |
|-----------|-----------|-----------|----------|-----------|
| *herald* | September | thirty | 1862 | *for* |
| Adam | period | I | received | last |
| evening | your | dispatch | suspend-ing | my |
| removal | from | command | out | of |
| a | sense | of | public | duty |
| I | shall | continue | to | discharge |
| the | duties | of | my | command |
| to | the | best | of | my |
| ability | until | otherwise | ordered | Arabia |
| | *Seward* | | | *worst* |

Ignoring the opening word 'regulars' and starting with 'ordered', it is obvious that the message had been written by reading the plain text up the fourth column, down the third, up the fifth, down the second and up the first. Reading across the columns and ignoring the nulls (the words in italics), the descrambled message now makes sense. Only three words remain obscure—the words with capital letters, Lincoln, Adam and Arabia. These are codewords hiding the names of real people and places. They were contained in a secret Washington code-list. Lincoln was Louisville, Kentucky, Adam was General Halleck, Union commander-in-chief, and Arabia was General Buell, fighting the enemy in central Kentucky.

Union prisoners, held captive in Confederate gaols, used the simple Pig-Pen cipher to communicate with friends outside. The alphabet is written in a nine-cell diagram (Fig. 12).

| ABC | DEF | GHI |
|-----|-----|-----|
| JKL | MNO | PQR |
| STU | VWX | YZ  |

Fig. 12

Each letter of a plain-text message is indicated by the relevant section of the diagram plus one dot for the second letter, two dots for the third and no dot at all for the first. So, the message DANGER is written:

⊔ ⊐ · ⊏ ⊔ · ⊡

It is a very ancient cipher but, as a means of modern communication, it is probably most suitable for schoolboys.

By 1880, an extensive knowledge of code and cipher was considered a military necessity. A good, secure means of swift communication could give greater military or diplomatic advantage than ever before. Old methods were no good. New ones were essential.

The French produced the St-Cyr, a brilliant cipher named after the newly established military academy where it was invented. It was based on its great French predecessor, the Vigenère, but did away with that system's clumsy necessity for writing down complex alphabet tables and the danger that the encipherer would let his attention wander and lose his way amongst the maze of letters. To make a mistake with the St-Cyr is almost impossible. It consists of three alphabets arranged on a simple sliding device, as shown in Fig. 13.

Fig. 13

38

If the key-letter is J, then the lower alphabets are slid along until the J stands directly under the A of the top alphabet. The letters of the top alphabet stand for the plain text. The cipher equivalents are those letters of the movable alphabets immediately underneath. Thus if the key-letter is J, the plain-text message ADVANCE will be enciphered RUMRETV. If it is Q, KNFKXMO. The cipher changes as frequently as the key-letter, which the French usually changed every twenty-four hours.

The St-Cyr was the first cipher that supplied the three military essentials—simplicity, security and speed.

The British, in contrast to the sophistication of the French, were fighting the Boer War with their secret messages written in Latin. It was assumed that British officers had one thing in common—a classical education. However, whilst the average schoolboy's attainment in Latin was sufficient to fool the Boers, it fooled most of the British officers as well. To avert intelligence disaster, the British came up with probably the simplest and most effective substitution cipher ever devised—the Playfair.

This cipher is based on a key-word which is placed in the first positions of a squared alphabet from which the letter J has been omitted. (Any J in a message is enciphered I.) A completed square, with the key-word BRIGHTON, is shown in Fig. 14.

| B | R | I | G | H |
|---|---|---|---|---|
| T | O | N | A | C |
| D | E | F | K | L |
| M | P | Q | S | U |
| V | W | X | Y | Z |

Fig. 14

A message is divided into two-letter groups. If there are an

39

odd number of letters, the message is completed with a null:

SE  ND  RE  IN  FO  RC  EM  EN  TS  NO  WX

Messages are enciphered in these two-letter groups. To find the cipher equivalents of the first group, SE, find their position on the Playfair square, regard them as opposite corners of an imaginary square, and replace them with the two letters at the other two corners: KP. K in the same column as the original S, P in the same column as E. Similarly, ND becomes FT. RE is treated differently, as the two letters are in the same column: they are enciphered by the letters immediately under each—OP. IN, similarly, becomes NF. The next five groups are: FO—NE; RC—OH; EM—PD; EN—OF; and TS—MA. The next group, NO, is different again, as the letters are in the same line of the square. In this case they are enciphered by the letters immediately to their right, AN. Finally, W with its null X to make a two-letter group are again in the same line, so are replaced by the letters to their right, XY. This gives the completed message:

Plain text:   SE  ND  RE  IN  FO  RC  EM  EN  TS  NO  WX
Cipher text:  KP  FT  OP  NF  NE  OH  PD  OF MA  AN  XY

The process can be additionally complicated by, for example, making every fourth letter of the original message a null.

The key-word, and thus the organisation of the whole square, is changed at a pre-arranged time every day—even every hour. In this way, any codebreaker who has succeeded in working out the current key-word will soon find all his efforts wasted when the key-word is changed.

Another British cipher, brought up to date and used at this time, was Wolseley's square—named after the 19th century commander-in-chief of the British Army, General Sir Garnet

Wolseley. Like Playfair, it is based on a square, uses a key-word and omits J (Fig. 15, where the key-word is CAREFUL).

| 1 | 2 | 3 | 4 | 5 |
|---|---|---|---|---|
| C | A | R | E | F |
| 8 | 9 | 10 | 11 | 6 |
| U | L | B | D | G |
| 7 | 12 | | 12 | 7 |
| H | I | K | M | N |
| 6 | 11 | 10 | 9 | 8 |
| O | P | Q | S | T |
| 5 | 4 | 3 | 2 | 1 |
| V | W | X | Y | Z |

Fig. 15

Each letter is numbered and each number occurs twice, the two numerical sequences curling distinctively into the middle of the square, where the central letter is not numbered at all. Encipherment is simple. Message: ENEMY SIGHTED. E on the square is numbered 4. The other number 4 governs the letter W, so E is enciphered W. And so on. If the un-numbered K is in a message, it is enciphered as itself, K. The completed encipherment reads:

Plain text:   E N E M Y   S I G H T E D
Cipher text:  W H W I A   L M O N U W P

As with Playfair, the cipher can be changed merely by altering the key-word.

This outburst of cryptographic activity in the second half of the nineteenth century not only refined cryptographic techniques but also showed when it is best to use a code, and when a cipher. What determines the choice is the need for maximum security in a particular situation.

Broadly speaking, diplomats and the navy prefer a code because they are based in one place, an embassy or a ship, and they can work with the aid of a complicated codebook behind locked doors without fear of intrusion. Spies and the army, on the other hand, prefer cipher. They are constantly on the move, have neither time nor security to work from a heavy and suspicious object like a codebook, and need something that gives maximum security with minimum paper-work. Ciphers, based on key words which can be carried in the head, are ideal.

Just how ideal is proved by the case of General Gordon, trapped by the Sudanese on 12 March 1884 in the city of Khartoum. Gordon was safe until the defensive waters of the Nile fell sufficiently for the enemy to attack. To preserve his government's secrets, he dispatched all his codebooks on the last boat to leave the city. From then on, secret communication with the world outside was impossible. And secret plans for Khartoum's relief, smuggled into the city in his own code, Gordon could no longer read. But if he had used a cipher which he could have committed to memory, he would have had no problems, read the plans, acted on them, and saved himself, his army and a quarter of a million square miles. As it was, just before the arrival of the relief forces, Khartoum fell and Gordon was killed. It was the high price he paid for using code in a cipher situation.

# 5     Codebreakers

In the first half of the nineteenth century, intelligence activity concentrated on inventing codes; in the second half, it began to pay as much attention to breaking them. This shift of emphasis was due to the work of a German officer, Major Kasiski. The historical reason for the lack of interest in code-breaking was simply that no one knew how to do it. The Vigenère cipher, now nearly three hundred years old, was still thought to be impregnable. It was Kasiski who showed how to break it, and his method has become the corner-stone of all modern analysis.

It was already known that, in every language, certain letters occur more frequently than others. In English, German, French and Spanish the most frequently used letter is E. In English alone, the most common letters are ETAONRIS—which can easily be remembered by the ominous sounding phrase A SIN TO ER.

The frequency table on page 44, showing the occurrence of letters in English, is typical of the tables used by analysts.

What Kasiski showed was that, in all languages, besides single letters appearing frequently, certain combinations of letters appear frequently as well. In English, the most frequently recurring double letters (called bigrams) are TH (168 times in 1,000 words), HE (132), AN (92), RE (91), ER (88), IN (86), ON (71), AT (68), and ND (61). The most

| Letters | *Frequency of occurrence in 1,000 words* | *Frequency of occurrence in 1,000 letters* |
|---|---|---|
| 1 | E | 591 | 131.05 |
| 2 | T | 473 | 104.68 |
| 3 | A | 368 | 81.51 |
| 4 | O | 360 | 79.95 |
| 5 | N | 320 | 70.98 |
| 6 | R | 308 | 68.32 |
| 7 | I | 286 | 63.45 |
| 8 | S | 275 | 01.01 |
| 9 | H | 237 | 52.59 |
| 10 | D | 171 | 37.88 |
| 11 | L | 153 | 33.89 |
| 12 | F | 132 | 29.24 |
| 13 | C | 124 | 27.58 |
| 14 | M | 114 | 25.36 |
| 15 | U | 111 | 24.59 |
| 16 | G | 90 | 19.94 |
| 17 | Y | 89 | 19.82 |
| 18 | P | 89 | 19.82 |
| 19 | W | 68 | 15.39 |
| 20 | B | 65 | 14.40 |
| 21 | V | 41 | 9.19 |
| 22 | K | 19 | 4.20 |
| 23 | X | 7 | 1.66 |
| 24 | J | 6 | 1.32 |
| 25 | Q | 5 | 1.22 |
| 26 | Z | 3 | 0.77 |

frequent triple letters (trigrams) are; CON, ENT, ERS, EVE, FOR, HER, ING, TED, TER, THE, TIO and VER. These discoveries led to others. For example, more than half of all English words begin with A, O, S, T, or W. More than half end in D, E, S, or T. The most frequent endings for British surnames are SON, TON, ER, FORD, MAN and BY. The most frequently used English words are 'the', 'of', 'and' and 'to', and the most repeated noun is 'today'. Kasiski also pointed out that it is impossible to write a long message without these repetitions. And recognising and counting these repetitions is how the code is eventually broken. The code-breaker is called a cryptanalyst—an analyst of *kryptos*, secrets.

Presented with a coded message (cryptogram), and without any idea of how it was enciphered, the cryptanalyst can make a number of assumptions. If the letters A SIN TO ER occur frequently, he is dealing with a transposition. That is because a transposition cipher, remember, only rearranges the letter order. It does not change the letters themselves, so the most frequently used letters and words in a message remain the same. If, however, the A SIN TO ER letters occur very rarely, then the cipher is a substitution, as the object of a substitution is to replace the letters with others. So if the cryptogram has Z and Q as its most frequent letters, it is obvious that they stand for something else—probably E or T.

Without frequency tables a solution is almost impossible. They are so important that they can help expert codebreakers break ciphers in any language—even Chinese and even when the analyst cannot understand the Chinese symbols.

As well as frequency tables, codebreakers need high intelligence and an enquiring mind. As well as that, they need patience and accuracy, for, whilst intuition and experience play their part, codes are broken through the absolute mastery of the characteristics of language and a determination to work according to a strict plan. The work can be exciting when moving towards a solution but, for the most part, it is a routine chore that is as frustrating as it can be absorbing. Hans Fischer, a German cryptanalyst of World War II:

Obviously staring at something which is completely meaningless and doing that for hours and days and sometimes weeks on end can be extremely boring. You may well go to sleep doing it. On the other hand you have to be alert all the time. It's a tremendous strain, a psychological and nervous strain. You get into the attitude where you see letters and figures everywhere and try to read a meaning into them. Car numbers. Telephone numbers. If they begin with 66 and end with 44 then you think that must have some significance. It's with you all the time. You can't escape it. It almost sends you mad.

In World War II it really did send men mad. One of the brightest men in the American intelligence service, after completing the most important break of his whole career, was in hospital for a year suffering from physical and nervous exhaustion. Another spent six years in a mental hospital. It is a measure of the difficulty of their profession.

By 1900, as a result of Kasiski's discoveries, no code or cipher was safe from expert analysis. All that Intelligence could hope for was to delay decipherment till the secret information revealed was no longer of value. In order to achieve this, encoding techniques became more complex. But complexity led to mistakes, and it was simple encoding mistakes that led to the major intelligence disasters of World War I.

# 6 *The Zimmerman Telegram*

World War I was a vast code and cipher battle that the combatants had been preparing for over thirty years. It was finally lost and won as the result of codebreaks.

In the middle of January 1917, Room 40, the codebreaking branch of British Naval Intelligence, intercepted a coded telegram. Decoded, it read:

> Berlin. Foreign Office, January 16th 1917. Most secret. For your excellency's personal information . . . we . . . propose to begin . . . unrestricted submarine warfare . . . submarines will compel England to peace in a few months. Acknowledge receipt. Zimmerman

It was sent by the German Foreign Minister, Arthur Zimmerman, to his ambassador in Washington. Of course, when it arrived in Room 40, it was in code and unreadable. But its decoding turned out to be probably the most important single solution in intelligence history.

Room 40, named after the number of the room in the Admiralty, Whitehall, in which it was housed, came into existence almost by accident. Early in 1914 the British Post Office was picking up coded foreign wireless signals which it did not know what to do with. It offered them to the Admiralty. But the Admiralty did not know what to do with them either. The

Director of British Naval Education realised that they were German naval messages containing invaluable secret information. The trouble was that no one knew how to decode them and extract the secrets. So the Director went to the British Museum Library and taught himself the principles of cryptanalysis. Room 40, successor to Walsingham's intelligence service, had begun.

Later the same year, this embryonic intelligence department had a stroke of luck. The German cruiser *Magdeburg* was sunk by the Russians, and in classic intelligence style the German captain ordered the ship's codebooks to be thrown overboard. A few hours later, the Russians fished up the body of a German seaman. Clasped in the dead man's arms was a German signalbook. Unlikely as it now seems, the Russians handed the book over to the British, and Churchill, then the First Lord, 'received from the hands of our loyal allies these sea-stained priceless documents'.

And priceless they were. From a detailed examination of them, the Admiralty learnt the nature of the German naval signals, and, after a little practice, were able to read nearly all German naval codes for the rest of the war. It meant, for example, that before the important battle of Jutland, the codebreakers in the corridors of Whitehall knew the exact position of every German ship before the battle even started.

To intercept the German navy's wireless traffic, Britain was ringed by listening posts. Here, quite by accident, Room 40 began to pick up German diplomatic traffic as well. This was quite an embarrassment to the British Establishment. Despite the enormous political and tactical advantage that the possession of such German messages would give, the idea of Britain deliberately eavesdropping on the other chap's cables was out of the question. It might be war, but it wasn't cricket. So Room 40 officially had to close its ears—and listen in private.

As the importance of the work increased, so did the number

of codebreaking personnel—an incredible assortment of people who had either the most tenuous connections with the Admiralty, or no connections at all. People like Edward Molyneux, later to become famous as a fashion designer; Desmond MacCarthy, writer and critic; Nigel de Grey, publisher; and numerous young academics like Walter Bruford—'My former teacher at Cambridge was looking for fresh recruits for Room 40 and he asked me if I would like to go, and so I went'. Or Leonard Willoughby—'I thought it was some sort of office work, connected with my subject—German. Later I discovered, of course, what was expected of me.' Even in this hitherto all-male preserve, women. Miss May Jenkin, later 'Aunt Elizabeth' of the BBC's 'Children's Hour'—'They were looking for somebody who knew German, and as I'd always been very keen about the Navy, I had a brother in it, I applied and did a bit of translation and that was that and I went in about a week later.' These people, initially untrained, haphazardly recruited, were, in the words of Admiral James, later head of Room 40, 'perhaps the most brilliant lot of young people ever brought together'. From the civilised surroundings of Whitehall, these young people, as Britain struggled to gain the intelligence advantage, conducted their secret war.

Willoughby: 'One felt that Room 40 was a pivot of information on which the safety of the country depended.' James: 'Messages were coming in the whole time, sometimes like a Maxim gun. And there were fellows receiving them and separating them and giving them out to the different departments.' Jenkin: 'We were all engaged on decoding and the messages were brought in in large numbers and we all had some on our desks. And there were thirty words that had been found, you see, and you wrote them in and then you struggled with the rest of the meaning.'

The success of Room 40 was largely due to the man who ran it, Admiral William Reginald Hall. 'Blinker' Hall, who had a nervous habit of blinking, was fearless, self-confident—and ruthless. It was Hall who provided the evidence to convict Sir Roger Casement, the former British consul who tried to raise rebellion in Ireland in 1916. Room 40 intercepted a message from Berlin that said Casement would be landed, by German submarine, on the coast of Ireland. His departure would be signalled by the codeword OATS. When, on 12 April, Room 40 intercepted a cable with the word OATS in it, the police were informed and Casement arrested as he came ashore at Tralee Bay. He was tried, convicted of high treason and shot. It was Hall, too, who trapped Mata Hari. The German naval attaché in Madrid cabled Berlin requesting money and instructions for agent H-21. Berlin ordered the agent to Paris. Hall intercepted the order, broke the code and passed the information to the French. Agent H-21, better known by her stage name Mata Hari, was picked up and shot by a twelve-man firing squad.

But, most important, it was Hall who broke the Zimmerman telegram and put the Allies on the road to victory.

By late 1916, just before Zimmerman sent his telegram, the war between Britain and Germany had reached stalemate. In the trenches of the Western Front, the two sides fought backwards and forwards over the same stretch of mud: gaining two miles as they lost two million men. In the North Sea the British had effectively bottled up the German Fleet after the battle of Jutland, but in the North Atlantic German submarines coninued to sink British merchant ships.

The German plan was simple—to starve Britain into defeat. The country to help Britain was America, but the Americans were in no mood to get involved in a far-off European war. Britain would have to go it alone. So far, sinking British merchant ships had not brought the Germans victory, as a lot of Britain's food came in neutral American vessels. The Germans needed to sink them as well, but they ran the risk of the

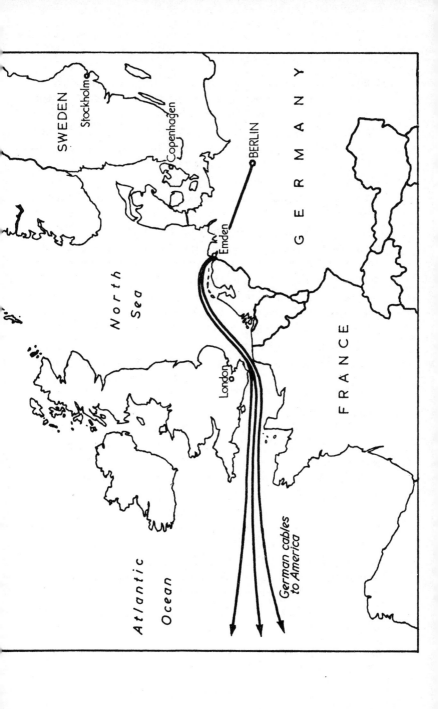

United States' declaring war on the German empire. This was the one thing Britain wanted, the one thing the Germans wanted to avoid. But the American anti-war mood worked in Germany's favour, and there was the encouraging precedent of the *Lusitania*. Sunk by a German submarine in 1915, the 128 American dead had not been sufficient to bring the United States into the war. The Germans decided to gamble. They would unleash their full U-boat power in the North Atlantic.

To keep America from entering the war, Arthur Zimmerman, the German Foreign Minister, devised a plan that would keep the Americans so busy elsewhere that they would have neither the time nor the equipment to help the Allies. But Zimmerman's immediate problem was how to get his secret plan to his ambassador in Washington.

The German telegraph cables, which carried German diplomatic traffic, ran directly from Berlin, out to sea near Emden, along the Channel bed and so across the Atlantic to America. On 5 August 1914, the very first day of the war, a British cable ship called the *Telconia* had grappled up the German cables, cut them and dropped them back, useless, into the water. It was Britain's first offensive action of the war and had the unforeseen result, three years later, of posing Zimmerman his major problem.

He had two possible courses of action. The first was to send his message on the 'Swedish Roundabout'. This was the nickname the British gave to the Swedish cable route that went from Berlin, to Stockholm, then, via the Canary Islands, Cape Verde Islands and Ascension Island, to the Argentine. The Swedes carried the German traffic as far as South America, where the cables were delivered to the German Embassy in Buenos Aires. Here they were transferred to German routes and forwarded to Mexico City and Washington—a circuitous route of 7,000 miles.

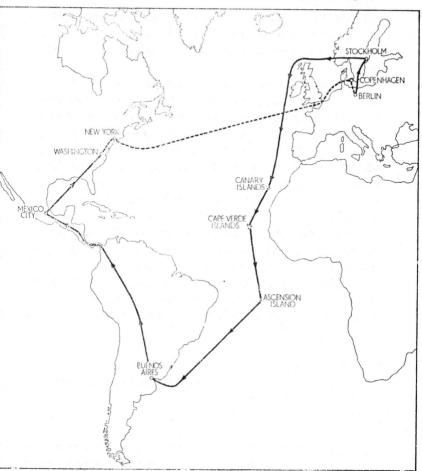

Zimmerman's other option was to send his message direct to Washington on American diplomatic cables. It was a much more direct route and ran from Berlin to Copenhagen, then across the Atlantic to New York and Washington. The rather gullible Americans had taken the unprecedented step of allowing their cables to be used by the Germans as an act of friendship, believing the German messages contained peace proposals. But it was an agreement that nearly led to America's undoing.

Zimmerman, to make sure his message arrived, sent it both ways. But what he did not appreciate was that both cables touched England, and in England his messages were intercepted by Room 40. On duty, the night the cables arrived hot from the telegraph wires, were Nigel de Grey and the Rev. William Montgomery. It was a very long message and written, James-Bond-like, in code Double 'O' Seven—Five. Code 0075 was one of a number of diplomatic codes that the Germans had recently introduced to their priority embassies throughout the world. It was a two-part code—consisting of 10,000 different groups of numbers representing 10,000 different words. The linking of a particular number with a particular word was purely arbitrary. There was no numerical or alphabetical order; everything was in scrambled order and was, in effect, a giant monalphabetic substitution. When it arrived, the telegram looked something like this:

```
0158 0075 4280 6321 9206 1783 5841 7390 8214 4569 4099 1439
3366 2479 4367 1783 4111 0652 5310 1139 8436 1284 9088 2895
2785 1139 8636 5731 7100 5224 8888 2785 2834 7009 1783 4852
4099
```

The task that faced Montgomery and de Grey was enormous. But it was not their first 0075 cable, and they already had a well-established working method. They guessed that the opening number-groups of the message followed a regular pattern, and they were right. The first numbers were for identification. 0158—the number of the telegram; 0075—the code used (so that the recipient could decode it); 4280—the telegram's source, the Berlin Foreign Office; the fourth and fifth groups were the date the cable was sent, which was obvious—16 January.

The next job was to isolate the stops. For a message to make sense, punctuation is essential. But how to find it? Number groups at the end of a telegram are obvious candidates. 4099 proved to be a stop. So did 1783. Full stops and words used frequently in messages always have more than one code group, as they would otherwise be too easily recognised by the code-breakers. But the code-clerks, the men who actually send the cables, get bored and lazy and memorise only one or two alternative number groups, repeating them over and over again, and jeopardising the security of the entire code. Montgomery and de Grey marked in the repeated stops 4099, 1783. 2785. And so, with all the stops marked in, the structure of the message began to appear.

0158 0075 BERLIN FOREIGN OFFICE JANUARY 16th STOP 5841 7390 8214 4569 STOP 1439 3366 2479 4367 STOP 4111 0652 5310 1139 8436 1284 9088 2895 STOP 1139 8636 5731 7100 5244 8888 STOP 2834 7009 STOP 4852 STOP

The cable, of course, was written in German. De Grey and Montgomery needed to have a perfect knowledge of the language in order to understand the cable at all, but it was the idiosyncrasies of German syntax, the actual order of German words, that were to provide the next clue. English and German word order are quite different. In German, a verb usually comes at the end of a sentence. English: 'I went for a walk'. German: 'I for a walk went.' So, in this German cable, the word immediately before a stop is probably a verb—like 7009 —BESTATIGEN which means ACKNOWLEDGE. Other verbs were 8888—ZWINGEN—COMPELLED; and 2895—BEGINNEN —BEGIN.

If, at the end of a message, there is a group of figures separated by two stops, as here, it is probably a signature. From a knowledge of previous messages stockpiled in Room 40 from the Swedish roundabout, they recognised the name 4852—ZIMMERMAN.

Every trade and profession has its own cliché language. Business letters, for example: 'Thanking you for your esteemed letter of the 14th inst.' Encoded, this would be a certain give-away, as it is easy to guess. Diplomacy has its give-away jargon, too: high-flown and full of 'imperial ministers' and 'your excellency's' and smacking of monocle and court etiquette. So, before diplomats realised this, diplomatic messages usually began with a standard preamble, and pompous Arthur Zimmerman's messages were no exception. 5841—MOST SECRET —7390—YOUR EXCELLENCY'S—8214—PERSONAL—4569—INFORMATION.

As the result of months of work spent on previous 0075 messages, Montgomery and de Grey were able to edit out other words until the cable looked like this:

0158 0075 BERLIN FOREIGN OFFICE JANUARY 16th STOP MOST SECRET YOUR EXCELLENCY'S PERSONAL INFORMA-TION STOP TO IMPERIAL MINISTER IN 2479 HAND STOP INTEND UNRESTRICTED SUBMARINE WARFARE FEBRUARY 1st TO BEGIN STOP SUBMARINES ENGLAND TO PEACE FEW MONTHS COMPELLED STOP RECEIPT ACKNOWLEDGE STOP ZIMMERMAN STOP

It was only a partial solution, but what Hall was given was enormously significant. It confirmed what Britain already feared—Germany was about to unleash her submarine power, but somehow keep America from joining the war.

Hall took the partly de-coded telegram to Balfour, the British Foreign Secretary. Balfour, unable to decide what to do, passed the buck and told Hall to deal with the thing himself. Hall was forced to become politician, strategist and spy. His only weapon, an incomplete telegram on which the whole of Britain's future might depend.

As the message promised, Germany started unrestricted submarine warfare on 1 February 1917. The American answer was to break off diplomatic relations. They did not, as Hall hoped, declare war. The only way to jerk America out of her isolation and into the war was for Hall to tell the Americans the German plan to keep the United States occupied if she *did* declare war.

Hall guessed what the plan was. There was a clue in the telegram. 'Hand to Imperial Minister in 2479.' What and where was 2479? Hall guessed it was Mexico. Could it be that Germany planned to keep America occupied in a war with Mexico? Drawing American troops to defend her southern border, leaving no one to fight the Germans elsewhere? It seemed plausible—and very clever.

The temptation for Hall to reveal his hunch was tremendous. That he did not do so is a tribute to his cool nerve and ability as a statesman. He could imagine the popular American outcry if he could prove what Germany was up to—but he had not got the proof. The Americans would dismiss his story as a clumsy piece of British propaganda; and, to have played his hand too early, would have meant throwing away his trump card. It would also have meant revealing British Intelligence methods to no purpose. Hall could not afford to tell the world of the existence of Room 40, as this would have alerted every cable-sending nation to the possibility of British interception. He could not reveal, either, that he had code 0075 because the Germans would have changed the code and a vital source of Room 40 information would have dried up. And he could not reveal that he was tapping Swedish cables: the

Americans would soon guess he was tapping American cables as well—and he could not afford to upset the Americans.

Hall needed two things—proof of the German intentions and a cover story that would conceal the real workings of British Intelligence. His plan was brilliantly simple. If 2479 really was Mexico, then the German ambassador in Washington would have forwarded the contents of Zimmerman's telegram to the German consul there. If Hall could find a copy of the telegram in Mexico City it might reveal further information and would also mean, when Hall published the cable, that enquiring German and American eyes would be firmly focused thousands of miles away from London and Room 40. The only way for Hall to find the telegram was to steal it.

The commercial telegraph cables of the Western Union Telegraph Office, cables that the diplomatic service used, ran directly from Washington to Mexico. As telegraph offices always kept a copy of all cables sent on their lines, including ones in code, the place to look for Zimmerman's telegram was in the Mexico City Telegraph Office.

A British agent called 'T' broke into the office and, rifling through the files, discovered, as Hall expected, a copy of the Zimmerman telegram forwarded by the German ambassador in Washington to his colleague in Mexico. As the Mexican consulate was not one of Germany's top diplomatic posts, the consul there had not been issued with the top secret code 0075. So the Washington ambassador had forwarded the telegram translated into a code the Mexican consul could understand—code 13042.

It was a bad code—easy to crack. The alphabetical sequence of words was directly paralleled by the number order. The numbers ran in sequence for several words at a time and only changed every so often. From words actually recovered from the Mexico City version of the Zimmerman telegram, the code looked like this:

| | |
|---|---|
| 13605 | Februar |
| 13732 | fest |
| 13850 | finanzielle |
| 13918 | folgender |
| 17142 | Frieden |
| 17149 | Friedensschluss |
| | etc. |

So when Room 40 discovered that 'Februar' was 13605 and 'finanzielle' was 13850, it was a pretty good bet that 13732 was a word that lay alphabetically somewhere between the two. Of course, this kind of assumption was not possible in 0075 where the order of words and numbers never follow in sequence. For Room 40, reading the Mexican cable was simple as they had most of code 13042 already—it had been a regular code on the Swedish Roundabout for years. And Hall was helped by a major encoding mistake made by the German ambassador in Washington. It is a basic encoding safeguard if you are sending a message on in another code, *never* to send the message in exactly the same words. If you do, and both versions of the message fall into the hands of a spy, cross-reference between one code and another makes the solution of the message that much simpler. Which is what happened with the Zimmerman telegram. The unreadable parts in code 0075 were broken merely by referring to the message in the readable 13042.

The vital codegroup 2479 was, as Hall had guessed all along, MEXICO. More than that, the message in code 13042 now revealed the full extent of Zimmerman's plan. Mexico would attack the United States and, in return for her help, receive the American states of Arizona, Texas and New Mexico. Better than Hall could have hoped for! He passed the information to President Wilson, with the cover story, for both American and German consumption, that the telegram had been 'obtained' in Mexico and code 13042 'obtained' very early in the war.

The American newspapers carried banner headlines. Suddenly war fever gripped America as the news sank in that Germany actually planned to hand over parts of the United States to Mexico. Incredibly, Wilson still hesitated. Was it a British plot? Hall's proof was not sufficient. Wilson wanted further evidence.

Fortunately, Hall had it. He suggested that, as Zimmerman had sent his message on American diplomatic cables, Wilson might find an original copy of the telegram in the United States itself. And there it was, sitting un-decoded in the files of the State Department. The Americans had acted as the German errand boy and carried a message that contained plans for their own destruction. It is probably the only time in history that such a thing has happened. The Americans, of course, could not read the cable and Hall had to decode it for them. Wilson was at last convinced and, on 2 April 1917, signed the declaration of war against Germany. And, if further proof were needed, Arthur Zimmerman actually owned up to sending the cable in the first place.

From amateurish, stumbling beginnings, Hall had converted Room 40 into one of the most successful cryptanalytical units in intelligence history, its greatest success the decoding of the Zimmerman telegram. In the words of Admiral Sir William James: 'I think it altered the whole course of history. It was the arrival of the large American army in France and the large addition to our naval forces by the whole American navy, that really turned the war in our favour.'

# 7             *ADFGX*

Despite the brilliance of Room 40 and the breaking of the Zimmerman telegram, the Allies had not been having everything their own way. The Germans themselves had a more than competent cryptanalytic service, and had charted up their own considerable successes. They had broken the British Playfair method and most of the codes used by the French, but their first major achievement was not so much the result of innate German ability as of Russian incompetence.

The First and Second Russian armies, early in 1914, were operating in what is now Poland. Divided by several inhospitable miles, they communicated by radio. Aware that the Germans had broken their old ciphers, the Russians had carefully built up a new and complicated cipher that would hopelessly confuse the Germans as soon as it was brought into use. The only copy of the cipher in existence was owned by General Jilinsky, who commanded the Second Army. He had given it to General Rennenkampf, commander of the First Army, and thus produced the ludicrous situation of the First Army sending messages in the new cipher to the Second Army which could not read them. In an attempt to re-establish communication between the two, the Second Army reverted to the old ciphers—but the First Army could not read these either as it had already destroyed the old keys. Chaos developed, with the Germans approaching.

The Germans were commanded by General Hindenberg. His force was small and, if the Russian armies joined up, he would be overwhelmed. Then, to his astonishment, his intelligence officer brought him an intercepted Russian message from General Rennenkempf to General Jilinsky. It read: 'Temporarily halting. Cannot join up as supply trains not arrived.' And it was written in clear. Was it a Russian trick to fool him? Further messages proved that it was not. The Russian generals, desperate and unable to communicate in cipher, had reverted to the ridiculously dangerous practice of sending messages in no code at all. Hindenberg, realising the Russian predicament, attacked. The battle of Tannenberg was over and the Russians routed in three days. It was one of the most decisive victories in history.

The Russians had some revenge when the *Magdeburg* was sunk and set in motion the chain of events that led to Room 40's Zimmerman telegram solution, but it was an isolated victory. Russian code security was as poor on the ocean as it had been on land. In the Black Sea, the Russian naval presence was large. The German presence was small—just three warships incapable of achieving anything against such powerful opposition. But even so, the Germans had the whip hand—they possessed most of the Russian naval codes, and knew how to take advantage of them. They sent out a message in Russian code to the Russian admiral: an order to take his warships to the eastern end of the Black Sea. With no reason to believe the message was not genuine, the admiral steamed off, leaving the Germans to sink the unprotected Russian merchant fleet and fire its harbours.

The Russians finally collapsed in 1917, and the withdrawal of Russia from the war jeopardised all the potential advantage gained by the coup of the Zimmerman telegram. As the Americans arrived in Europe, the German Western Front was suddenly reinforced by three million battle-hardened men transferred from Russia. The small American force could not redress the balance and, in early 1918, Britain and France faced defeat. What the Allies needed was time—time for the arrival of more Americans. What the Germans needed was to strike and strike hard before the Allies could be reinforced. On the Western Front itself, the exhaustion and stalemate of years were already working to German advantage. Any small Allied advance was at the expense of men they could ill afford. French divisions were skeletons of just 6,000 men. The British were now 100,000 men below strength and the once plentiful supply of Allied cannon-fodder had almost dried up. Morale was low; the Allied armies at their weakest. All along the front line the Germans were stronger than the Allies, outnumbering them by 200,000 men. What Erich von Ludendorff, the German leader, planned to do was break the line and march on Paris. If Paris fell, the war would end.

To have even the slightest chance of preventing a German breakthrough, the Allies needed to mass their strength at the exact point of the German attack, which could come anywhere. The only way of finding out where it would come was through a codebreak.

The Germans at the beginning of the war had made mistakes—had used simple codes that the French had easily cracked. They were determined not to make the same mistakes again and, to ensure the security of their planned big offensive, all references to German battle strategy were to be enshrouded in a completely new cipher. The form of the cipher was partly dictated by circumstances. It was needed to transmit orders along the battle front, quickly, accurately and with complete security. The standard of German radio operation, in morse, was poor. The old hands were dead. The new men had to have something easy. The job of devising the code was given to Colonel Fritz Nabel:

I knew from my own education in radiotelegraphy that certain letters were easier to transmit and receive in morse than others. And seven of these were especially simple: A D F G R V X. So I considered how to make a cipher out of these.

Nabel's cipher was both brilliant and simple. Called ADFGX, it was a combination of substitution and transposition. It had its precedents in the Greek square and Vigenère but was now brought up to date to suit the limited ability of the German signal clerks. The entire cipher was based on the most quickly and easily transmitted morse letters.

Nabel drew a grid and wrote the letters *adfgx* across the top and down the side. This gave him a square of twenty-five spaces. These spaces he filled out at random with the letters of the alphabet (Fig. 16). Part of the security of the code lay

|   | a | d | f | g | x |
|---|---|---|---|---|---|
| a | D | $^I/_J$ | N | F | S |
| d | H | A | O | G | E |
| f | R | Q | B | W | L |
| g | C | Y | M | U | V |
| x | Z | P | X | T | K |

Fig. 16

in the fact that the arrangement of letters in the square could be changed as often as necessary.

To encipher a message, the letters of the message are replaced by their letter equivalents on the side and top of the grid. For example, letter N would be enciphered *af*—*a* from the side column of the grid, *f* from the top. So, a short message (in English) would be enciphered:

| A | T | T | A | C | K | D | A | W | N | M | A | R | C | H |
|----|----|----|----|----|----|----|----|----|----|----|----|----|----|----|
| dd | xg | xg | dd | ga | xx | aa | dd | fg | af | gf | dd | fa | ga | da |

| T | W | E | N | T | Y | O | N | E | B | A | P | A | U | M | E |
|----|----|----|----|----|----|----|----|----|----|----|----|----|----|----|----|
| xg | fg | dx | af | xg | gd | df | af | dx | ff | dd | xd | dd | gg | gf | dx |

This substitution, in itself, gives no security whatever—A is always enciphered *dd*. But the next stage, the transposition, completely disguises the message by putting the code letters in a different order to conceal their original order.

Nabel began with a cipher key—a line of numbers written one to ten in jumbled order: 8 4 3 6 1 2 5 0 7 9. This key could also be changed frequently to confuse a codebreaker. (Note in passing how the cryptanalysts have learnt from Gordon of Khartoum. The German diplomats of the Zimmerman telegram used code, the German army here used cipher as the encipherers could remember the cipher key in their heads.)

In the columns under the cipher key, Nabel wrote out the letters of his enciphered message—writing across the page (Fig. 17). Notice that the bottom line of the table is not completely filled up. This was to prove the method's Achilles heel.

$$8 \; 4 \; 3 \; 6 \; 1 \; 2 \; 5 \; 0 \; 7 \; 9$$

| | | | | | | | | | |
|---|---|---|---|---|---|---|---|---|---|
| *d* | *d* | *x* | *g* | *x* | *g* | *d* | *d* | *g* | *a* |
| *x* | *x* | *a* | *a* | *d* | *d* | *f* | *g* | *a* | *f* |
| *g* | *f* | *d* | *d* | *f* | *a* | *g* | *a* | *d* | *a* |
| *x* | *g* | *f* | *g* | *d* | *x* | *a* | *f* | *x* | *g* |
| *g* | *d* | *d* | *f* | *a* | *f* | *d* | *x* | *f* | *f* |
| *d* | *d* | *x* | *d* | *d* | *d* | *g* | *g* | *g* | *f* |
| *d* | *x* | | | | | | | | |

Fig. 17

To send a message, letters are grouped in fives. Group one consists of the first five letters in column 1—*xdfda*. Group two, of the remaining letter in column 1 and the first four letters in column 2—*dgdax*. Group three, of the remaining letters in column 2 and the first three in column 3—*fdxad*. And so on, till all the letters are used up and the original message now reads:

*xdfda   dgdax   fdxad   fdxdx   fgddx   dfgad   ggadg   fdgad   xfgdx gxgdd   afagf   fdgaf   xg*

The last group is of only two letters—the Achilles heel still showing through. These five-groups are now transmitted in morse. The first group:    — ·· —   — ··   ·· —·   — ··   · —

At the front, the stalemate continued. The Allies needed to hold the line for at least another two or three months before the American build-up could become effective. This gave the Germans about ten weeks to win the war. The first indication the Allies had of the expected German offensive was when they intercepted a new and extremely complicated German cipher system. It was the first appearance of ADFGX—5 March 1918. The actual offensive occurred at 4 o'clock on 21 March with the greatest exhibition of fire-power the world had ever seen. After a furious military bombardment, sixty-two German divisions crashed forward on a forty-mile front. Within a week, the victorious German army had punched a hole thirty-eight miles deep in the Allied lines. The Western Front was broken.

Nabel's code had successfully concealed the German plans just as it would conceal future plans. The Allies, in the face of defeat, knew that a knowledge of ADFGX was essential to Allied survival.

The great race against time had begun. The Americans were arriving in France at the rate of 70,000 a week, fresh and ready for battle. Ludendorff had to attack again and reach

Paris before the full American strength could make itself felt. The new German attack was signalled by a fresh crop of intercepted ADFGX messages. The Germans considered their code indecipherable. Even Georges Painvin, France's most brilliant cryptanalyst, felt unable to solve it. But, at the end of one month, Painvin had made the break. A message intercepted on 1 April he solved by 5 April.

It is impossible to describe briefly how the break was made— but the clue came from the fact that the last transmitted group of a message was, as we have seen, rarely of five figures —usually four or two. This suggested to Painvin that the cipher was made up of pairs of letters and that each pair must represent one ordinary letter of the message. Furthermore, Painvin deduced that the only way in which five letters like *adfgx* can be made to do the work of twenty-five (or twenty-six) is on some sort of grid. Nabel's cipher had been betrayed by the Achilles heel of incomplete code groups.

Painvin's break appeared to supply the vital information that would bring the Allies success, but it did not, or not yet. It came too late to prevent the Germans from breaking through the line a second time—a giant pincer movement that brought the Germans within fifty miles of the French capital. Their forward positions were sufficiently close for the biggest gun the world had ever seen, Big Bertha, to land shells anywhere in the city. Shop-fronts were papered over to prevent damage from flying glass. Ministries prepared to evacuate. Food was expected to run short and housewives stockpiled food for the expected siege and final German breakthrough.

The Americans, now already arriving in Paris, gave renewed hope that the German tide could be stemmed. But dismal accounts, from the front, of increasing German strength and increasing Allied weakness made it very doubtful whether the Americans would reach the front line in sufficient numbers at all.

Ludendorff had about two weeks to make his final assault. It was his last chance. As on the two previous occasions, it was essential to attack the Allies where they would least expect it. Success depended on the security of ADFGX. What the Germans did not know was that Painvin had broken the code. The Germans, unsuspecting, prepared their final plans. The French intercepted the messages and—disaster—could not read them. The Germans had changed the cipher.

As well as the familiar five letters *adfgx* there was a sixth—*v*. The change itself was confirmation of the imminent German attack, but the Allies could now have no hope of stopping it. Paris would fall. The additional *v* seemed like a V for German victory. The chief reason for adding the sixth letter was to include numbers. Colonel Nabel had extended the original grid from twenty-five spaces to thirty-six. The additional eleven spaces were used for the letter *j* and the numbers 0-9 (Fig. 18).

|   | a | d | f | g | v | x |
|---|---|---|---|---|---|---|
| *a* | G | P | Y | M | B | T |
| *d* | 2 | Z | H | I | X | 4 |
| *f* | L | U | A | 7 | 1 | E |
| *g* | 5 | D | 6 | N | S | 9 |
| *v* | C | Ø | V | F | 8 | K |
| *x* | W | O | 3 | Q | J | R |

Fig. 18

This served to speed up the transmission of times and dates. For example, consider the message 'Attack dawn March twenty one Bapaume'. In the original cipher the date was written *gf dd fa ga da xg fg dx af xg gd*. In the improved cipher it was written *da fv*—the original eighteen cipher letters reduced to only four. And complete confusion amongst the Allies.

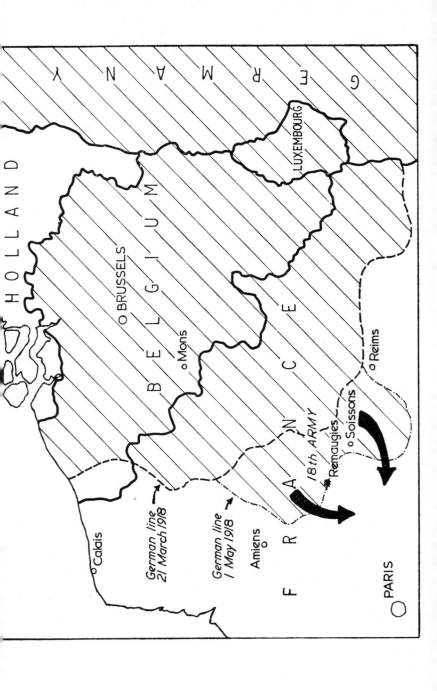

On the first operational day of the new code, Painvin, in the French Black Chamber, was fed more than seventy intercepted German messages. He made his triumph sound simple. 'I assumed that the extra pairs of letters must correspond to the first ten numbers. Fortunately, my hypothesis turned out to be correct.'

'We knew', said Nabel, 'that ADFGVX gave good security but we had no idea that such a clever man as Painvin was on the other side.'

On 2 June Painvin solved the most crucial message of the whole war. All it said was: 'Rush munitions STOP Even by day if not seen STOP'. Innocent enough—but it was addressed to the 18th German Army's General Staff at Remaugies, a tiny village half-way between the two arms of the German pincer that threatened Paris. It was a fair guess that Ludendorff was planning to hammer out the dent in the German lines.

The Allies acted at once. All available reserves were directed to the front. Troops already there were concentrated near Remaugies. Artillery, even cavalry. But the German positions remained strangely quiet. Could it be a German trick? Could Painvin's solution be wrong?

On 9 June the German offensive began. But it was not the Allies who were taken by surprise. For five days, the battle see-sawed then, gradually, the Allies began to advance. Ludendorff, under terrific pressure, called off the attack. For the Germans, time had run out—there was no chance to attack again. The war lasted another six months, but arriving American weight and improved Allied morale began to tell. To all intents and purposes, the greatest carnage the world had ever known was over.

Painvin himself gives credit to the army. 'The consequences were really, at bottom, that the Allied counter-attack had saved Paris and had achieved the first victory by the Allied armies in 1918.' But the credit is really Painvin's own. Room 40 and the Zimmerman telegram brought the Americans into the war. Painvin and ADFGVX gained the time for the Americans to become effective. Without these two codebreaks, the outcome of World War I could have been quite different.

# 8  Codes of the Underworld

The end of World War I was the beginning of the use of code and cipher by the underworld of organised crime. The codes they used were the commercial ones. These, which had been in regular use from the beginning of the century, looked like traditional codebooks and were rather bulky. They were not really secret as they were on open sale and were chiefly used by business firms to keep telegrams short and cheap. 'Managing director' as sixteen letters is three times as expensive to telegraph as its commercial code equivalent HAOMF or 72930. The codes gave some security, as not everyone could afford to buy them and they certainly prevented business secrets from becoming immediately public when committed to the public telegraph system. But it was not until the American Prohibition era, when the codes were taken over by the Mafia and similar business concerns, that the commercial codes were really used to hide secrets.

The criminal underworld has always used sign language. Marauding gangs who robbed and burned and terrorised fifteenth-century Europe had their own code signals which have come down to the twentieth century in the picture signs used by tramps. For example:

| Symbol | | Meaning |
|---|---|---|
| ﹏﹏ | (teeth) | Beware of the dog |
| O O O | (coins) | You might get money |
| ⊕ | (a hot-cross bun) | They will give you food |
| (cat symbol) | (a primitive cat) | Woman living alone |
| ⌀ | (a broken circle or broken head) | A good place to rob |

At the beginning of this century, the German criminologist Professor Hans Gross noticed a drawing on the wall of a church in Austria (Fig. 19). After studying it, he warned the local police to keep watch for anyone loitering near the building on Christmas Day, as he was sure they would be planning a break-in. The police watched, and, sure enough, picked up two men with long police records. Professor Gross explained:

It is all written on the wall of the church. The first drawing is the crude sketch of a parrot, made in a single line. That it's drawn in this way means that it's the signature of a criminal and that he's known as 'The Parrot'. The drawing of a church means the location, and the key that it is to be 'unlocked' or robbed. The drawing below is a crude representation of an infant in swaddling

Fig. 19

clothes. I assumed that this meant Christmas Day; and the three stones are a symbol for St. Stephen, who was stoned to death. St. Stephen's Day is December 26th; therefore the meaning of the whole thing is; 'The Parrot is going to burgle a church on December 26th. He wants someone to help him. Anyone who is willing, meet him near here on Christmas Day when the arrangements will be made.'

The men, presented with the evidence, admitted their guilt.

Sign language, though, was no good to the Mafia. Prohibition began in the United States in 1920 and produced one of the most violent and lawless periods in American history. During the thirteen years that it lasted it was illegal to manufacture, sell, or drink drink. Bars were closed, liquor imports banned. But the demand for alcohol remained steady, and disregard for the law became rampant. Small men like Al Capone saw their chance and propelled themselves into the world of big, though illegal, business. The speakeasies, the illegal bars in the cellars of downtown USA, brought a quick and easy profit. Drinks were small, but prices high, and the demand for bootleg-hootch increased. Most of the liquor came from gangland stills in the backrooms of warehouses. Conditions were primitive and unhygienic, and the number of deaths from alcohol poisoning rocketed—but so did profits.

The Federal Government, in a desperate attempt to enforce temperance, launched a campaign of burning, smashing and emptying every still and liquor bottle it could lay its hands on. The result was to drain America dry and force the gangsters onto the sea. Liquor must be smuggled from abroad. And it was the liquor flow from sea-going schooners that kept the whole criminal operation going. The most notorious of these twin-masted schooners was the *I'm Alone*. Built specially in 1924, she bought her liquor from the Melhado Bros in Belize, British Honduras, and sailed it the thousand miles across the

Caribbean to the United States. She dropped anchor in 'Rum Row'—the narrow strip of sea just outside the three-mile territorial waters limit where boats were safe from the American coastguard. Although she was Canadian registered, the Americans believed the *I'm Alone* was really an American boat.

To get their cargo ashore, the schooners relied on speedboats, and the schooner captains became masters of evasion. Trailed by a coastguard at night, they would fix their stern light to a buoy and drop it overboard. The coastguard would follow the light on the buoy whilst the smugglers disappeared in the opposite direction. Or they would despatch a decoy vessel—a speedboat that looked like the real thing but had nothing on board. While it was chased by the customs men, a second boat, loaded with liquor, could get away scot-free. When, as occasionally happened, it was obvious the customs men were going to board, the schooner captains still had an answer. The entire liquor cargo was tied in a net with glass floats and, with huge blocks of salt, sunk in the sea. Twenty-four hours later, the salt melted and up floated the cargo—with the coastguard well out of sight.

And there were dollar bills. To make sure the right people met the right boats the syndicate bosses tore a dollar bill and gave one half to the schooner captain and the other to the speedboat operator. As on a pound note, the dollar bill has a serial number on both sides of the paper, so, when the two boats met in Rum Row, the two strangers revealed their true identity to one another only if the numbers on the two halves of the dollar bill were the same.

Despite all these clever devices, there was still a communications problem. The schooners, afraid to enter territorial waters themselves, had to let the in-shore speedboats know that they had arrived. Similarly, the speedboats had to let the schooners know when the coast was clear. At first they used

light signals, but these were easily spotted. They used their
radios, but the coastguard listened in. So, predictably, they
turned to code. The coastguard still listened but could not
understand the codes; and, as the smuggling operations grew
and thousands of men and boats were involved, code became
more and more important. On one day a radio inspector heard
forty-five unlicensed radio stations broadcasting coded messages
within ten miles of New York. It gives some idea of the problem the authorities were up against and, to help them solve
the rum-running codes, they called in one of the nation's top
cipher experts, Mrs Elizabeth Friedman:

> The whole operation was extremely professional and the opera-
> tors highly security conscious. For one thing they never, ever
> put any plain text in their messages. One message I remember
> coming from shore to one of the big ships at sea said: 'Inform
> second mate wife has given birth to twins.' And back came the
> message all duly encoded in cipher, two or three or four or five
> stages, 'Second mate has no wife.' It was a laugh but they'd been
> careful to put it in code.

Although the smugglers' chief code sources were the un-secret
commercial codebooks, they invented a reasonably secure
method of use. The first step was to encode the plain text in
a commercial code called ABC, a code which, like all the
others, gave figure and letter equivalents for particular
phrases. The second step was to add 1000 to each code group.
For example:

Plain text: ANCHORED IN HARBOUR WHERE AND WHEN ARE
YOU SENDING FUEL.

| | | | |
|---|---|---|---|
| ABC code number: | 07033 | 52725 | 24536 |
| plus 1000: | 1000 | 1000 | 1000 |
| Final code group: | 08033 | 53725 | 25536 |

Step three was to turn to another codebook called ACME. It worked in the same way as all other commercial codebooks, but the figures and letters were different. In ACME, the letter equivalent of code group 08033 was BARHY. Similarly, 53725 and 25536 became OIJYS and WINUM. The final stage was to encipher everything again, including those words still left in plain-text. This was done by a simple monalphabetic substitution:

| | | | | | |
|---|---|---|---|---|---|
| A = J | | J = W | | S = H | |
| B = M | | K = I | | T = E | |
| C = N | | L = B | | U = G | |
| D = L | | M = X | | V = R | |
| E = T | | N = S | | W = Q | |
| F = O | | O = Z | | X = C | |
| G = U | | P = D | | Y = K | |
| H = A | | Q = V | | Z = P | |
| I = Y | | R = F | | | |

So the four stages of encipherment look like this:

| Plain text: | ANCHORED | IN HARBOUR | WHERE |
|---|---|---|---|
| ABC code: | 07033 | 52725 | |
| plus 1000: | 08033 | 53725 | |
| ACME code: | BARHY | OIJYS | |
| Substitution: | MJFAK | ZYWKH | QATFT |

| | | AND WHEN | ARE YOU | SENDING | FUEL |
|---|---|---|---|---|---|
| | | | 24536 | | |
| | | | 25536 | | |
| | | | WINUM | | |
| JSL | QATS | | QYSGX | | OGTB |

Sent in morse by ship-to-shore radio, it was intercepted by the coastguard and decoded by Mrs Friedman:

We could actually graph where the ships were by the particular code they were using. So we could almost draw a map of where these ships were at a given time.

In charge of a coastguard vessel was Lt Powell:

Most important to us was we knew where to run these vessels down; knew what they'd got on board and where they were planning to go.

Decoys and clever tricks no longer worked against the combined power of cryptanalysis and fast coastguard boats. The number of arrests at sea increased, but all attempts to catch the *I'm Alone* failed. In 1929 her job became more difficult when the United States extended her three-mile territorial waters limit to twelve. The rum-runners could no longer safely come close inshore and the coastguard kept a constant watch on the *I'm Alone* to pick up her ship-to-shore messages. But there weren't any. The owners of the *I'm Alone* were particularly clever. They behaved like genuine commercial code-users and sent all their messages from Belize to New York on the ordinary cables of the Western Union Telegraph Company. Then, in March 1929, the coastguard pounced. The *I'm Alone* was sighted in territorial waters off New Orleans, Louisiana, and Lt Powell was ordered to intercept. The schooner ran for the open sea. For three days and two hundred miles Lt Powell gave chase till the boat was cornered.

I ordered the master of the *I'm Alone* to stop his vessel, indicating that I wished to board him. And he indicated that he would not do so. These messages continued on for some little time, sometimes by signal, maybe semaphor. But it became clear that the Captain had no intention of stopping and I fired a blank or saluting shot at the bow. I believe I fired several of these shots. And no change of attitude apparently on the part of the skipper of the *I'm Alone*. So we just had to use the force that we had, which was gun-fire, and I directed my shells in through the hull, just above the water-line. It was a long time before I brought myself to firing below the water-line. But eventually I had to do that. The last shell that was fired tore a large hole in her side. And she settled quickly then. And went down.

The international outcry was enormous. The United States, on suspicion only, had sunk the vessel of a friendly power, Canada, and, more than that, she had done it in international waters. The Canadian government demanded an apology and a quarter of a million dollars in compensation. The Americans claimed the vessel was American-owned—but had no proof. They had to find it. All they knew was the date that the *I'm Alone* sailed from Belize.

Mrs Friedman, meanwhile, in the course of duty and quite by accident, had come across twenty-three telegrams sent from Belize to New York by the Western Union Telegraph Office. Her decodes were the start of some brilliant detective work.

The cable addresses used were CARMELHA for cables sent to Belize and MOCANA for cables to New York. It was just almost too obvious that Carmelha was a pronounceable number of letters made up from C. A. Melhado Brothers, the people who supplied all the liquor in Belize, British Honduras. Then I started to think about the cable address Mocana. And it seemed to me that the New York cables were obviously meant ultimately for Montreal, Canada. Mo Cana.

So far, so good. But no one yet had any inkling that the messages were connected with the *I'm Alone* nor could guess the significance of a Canadian cable address in New York. The messages looked like this:

YOJVY    RYKIP    PAHNY    KOWAG    JAJHA    FYNIG

Mrs Friedman soon recognised that they were written in a commercial code called Bentley. She looked up the code groups and discovered that the message meant: 'blank solve repairing her not nearly must leave feasible'. A nonsense message. But it had a sufficiently nautical flavour to rouse Mrs Friedman's suspicions. What she discovered was that someone had encoded his message not by using the code group in the column immediately opposite the plain text, but the group five places forward in the column. Revised accordingly, the unintelligible message made sense: 'Arrived. Some repairs necessary. Will leave Feb. 2nd.'

It was obviously the message of some unidentified rum-runner —but which one? The date, Feb. 2nd, provided the clue. In Belize, the US consul carefully recorded the amount of liquor loaded onto all suspect boats and logged the dates of sailing. When Mrs Friedman's decodes were read by the man in charge of the *I'm Alone* case, he saw that the dates of sailing and amount of liquor on board the unidentified vessel referred to in the cables corresponded exactly with the information recorded by the Belize consul for the *I'm Alone* when it left British Honduras on 2 February. Mrs Friedman's cables referred without doubt to the *I'm Alone*. The next step was to discover the boat's owner and prove he was not Canadian but American. The cable address 'Mocana' led through New York's violent underworld to the arrest of the man who received the telegrams. His name was Joseph Foran, really Dan Hogan, alias Dan Halpin, known to the police as the Al Capone of Louisiana, and head of a fifteen-million-dollar smuggling syndicate. Big Jim Clarke, the rum-runner's speedboat operator, tried to save his skin by turning evidence. Hogan, he claimed, had an address in Canada, but was a citizen of the United States. Suddenly the significance of the *I'm Alone* 'Mocana' cable address became apparent. Hogan, an American in New York, was having the cables sent on to his cover address in Montreal,

CANADA

Montreal

New York

USA

Washington

Rum Row

Rum Row

Telegraph cable

Rum Row

LOUISIANA

Atlantic Ocean

Galveston

New Orleans

M
E
X
I
C
O

Sunk
March 1929

GULF
OF MEXICO

Bahama
Islands

CUBA

Route of
'I'm Alone'

JAMAICA

HAITI

Belize
BRIT. HONDURAS

Pacific
Ocean

SOUTH
AMERICA

Canada. It was the proof the Americans had been looking for.

The evidence for the prosecution took five years to assemble. During that time, Hogan escaped from jail—twice—and Big Jim Clarke, lined up as chief prosecution witness, was shot. But eventually America had her proof, and at the subsequent hearing, international law was changed and history made. It was decided that a smuggling ship picked up inside territorial waters can be chased out to sea and, if necessary, sunk without infringing international law. It is a judgement that holds good to this day.

And Hogan went to jail—one of the thousands of rum-runners caught by the decoding techniques of the US coast-guard during Prohibition. As Mrs Friedman says: 'The decoded messages with their MOCANA cable address were the solid rock of the *I'm Alone* case. The facts were indisputable. Without the intercepted messages the case would not have been solved.' But the ultimate irony is that when Hogan went to jail, Prohibition, which had put him there, had already ended —two years before.

# 9 *To Catch a Spy*

In the late 1930s, as World War II seemed imminent, the nations of the world regrouped their intelligence services and prepared to carry on where they had left off in 1919. But things were to be different. It was to be a new kind of war and it demanded new and sophisticated techniques of intelligence to fight it. One of the major developments was the increasing use made by spies and other intelligence agents of a whole host of coding devices that did not operate on the usual method of numbers and letters at all.

There were plenty of historical precedents for this. Louis XIV of France issued all foreigners with a visa that cleverly concealed personal information that would be enormously helpful to anybody meeting the holder of the document for the first time. Lord John Hope, travelling to France in 1650, carried a visa written on oval-shaped yellow paper. The oval indicated that he was about thirty, the yellow, that he was English. Two small strokes under his name indicated that he was short and fat. A rose design in the paper, that he was genial; the fancy pattern round the edge, that he was rich, the comma after his name that he was a Protestant. Other marks showed whether he was intelligent, honest, stubborn or gullible. Such secret information would have alerted any Frenchman to Sir John's religious and political sympathies and have unmasked any impostor trying to travel on his documents.

At about the same time, Sir John Trevanion, a Royalist, was saved from certain death in Colchester castle by a letter from a friend.

> Worthie Sir John: – Hope, that is ye beste comfort of ye afflicted, cannot much, I fear me, help you now. That I would say to you, is this only: if ever I may be able to requite that I do owe you, stand not upon asking me. 'tis not much that I can do: but what I can do, bee ye verie sure I wille. I knowe that, if dethe comes, if ordinary men fear it, it frights you, accounting it for a high honour, to have such a reward of your loyalty. Pray yet that you may be spared this soe bitter, cup. I fear not that you will grudge any sufferings; only if bie submission you can turn them away, 'tis the part of a wise man. Tell me, an if you can, to do for you anythinge that you wolde have done. The general goes back on Wednesday. Restinge your servant to command – R.T.

On receipt of this letter, Sir John spent a day in meditation. In the evening he asked permission for an hour in the castle chapel, 'for privately repenting of my sins'. He spent the hour privately escaping, because the third letter after each punctuation mark spells a message: PANEL AT EAST END OF CHAPEL SLIDES.

Three hundred years later, in World War II, it was letters like these that were to provide one of the main forms of secret communication by spies and one of the main headaches for British censorship.

In late 1940, Britain had been driven out of Europe at Dunkirk and London was being blitzed. At the same time, over 3,000 miles away at the British censorship station in Bermuda, a letter was intercepted giving details of allied shipping in New York harbour. It was signed, innocently enough, 'Joe K'. Who was he? Why was he interested in Allied shipping? Was he an American? Was he German? With Britain in such dire straits, it was important for MI 6 to find out.

A spy usually keeps in touch with his spy master by radio. But this can be dangerous and unsatisfactory, and often the most secure way is to communicate by ordinary mail. To operate successfully, a spy must make no statement in his letter that might alarm a censor, or express himself in such a stilted way that it is obvious he is hiding a secret message. These pitfalls are not easily avoided. R.T.'s letter to Sir John Trevanion, for example, contained some curious and suspicious punctuation—especially the comma between 'bitter' and 'cup'. But, fortunately for Sir John, his Roundhead gaolers were not trained censors.

The Bermuda censorship station opened only a random 10 per cent of the mail, and the first Joe K letter was picked out by chance. Immediately it was suspect. The writer referred to guns on English shipping by the German term 'cannon'. So the writer was probably German, not American. The letter was addressed to Berlin—to a Herr Lothar Frederick. Investigation by British Intelligence showed that Lothar Frederick was a cover name for the Gestapo boss, Heinrich Himmler. So, Joe K was most probably an enemy agent operating a spy ring in the United States. And there was very little the British could do about it. America was still neutral. It was not against American law to send lists of Allied shipping anywhere; but it was against American law to tamper with the mail. Remembering the Zimmerman telegram and the importance of not upsetting the Americans, Britain had to tread carefully—particularly as she should not have been opening American mail in the first place.

The 'clippers'—the American flying-boats which carried the mail—could not manage the transatlantic hop without refuelling. They stopped at Bermuda, which made it the ideal place

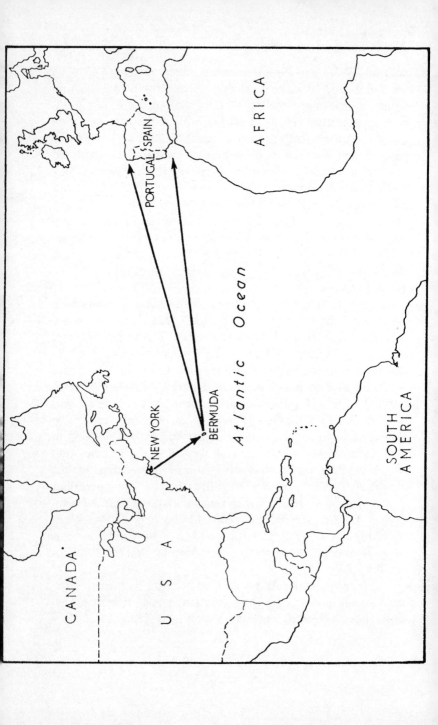

for Britain to investigate all letters travelling at speed between America and the German secret services in Europe. When the planes touched down at Darrel's Island, they were met by one of the chief censors, Miss Nadya Gardiner.

We sort of had a gentlemen's agreement to take the mail off, but apparently the clipper captains didn't join in that gentlemen's agreement and we had practically to take the mails off at gun point. Afterwards, we came to an agreement with the American Government that, providing the mails were not delayed more than 24 hours, they would permit us to take them off without resorting to force.

Miss Gardiner knew exactly what she was looking for.

We wanted to know what kind of information the enemy wanted. How much he knew, how he was getting it through, which secret groups were operating. And also how much the enemy already knew about what was being done. We were not in the least bit interested in any legitimate business correspondence. Mail was usually bagged for a specific country and we knew which countries we were interested in. There was obviously some mail that would be of no interest at all. And the rest would be routed to a very big sorting division which would do a very quick rough sort into what was obviously financial and trade mail, and personal mail. This would be sent up to the main censorship—grouped by languages, each of which was headed by a D.A.C., a deputy assistant censor. These censors had lists called watch lists of all firms known to trade with the enemy, of individuals known to have very strong German affiliations, and people who were genuinely suspect as pursuing actions inimical to the war effort. They would scan the mail quickly to see if there were any letters addressed to people on that watch list and, if there were, they would be given to special examiners who had been trained more thoroughly than the average examiner. Then, of course, the sorters also had photographs of certain mail to watch for, and this particular class of mail was exempt from the requirements that it were not delayed more than twenty-four hours because, very often, the tests and the examination and the analysis couldn't possibly be done in that time.

What were the censors looking for? Almost any unusual mark on the paper. Effective ciphers can be formed out of dots, lines, even zigzags. All the recipient needs is the order of the cipher alphabet. For example, a spy's code-name ROSEBUD can be written in three different ways, given the cipher alphabet in Fig. 20.

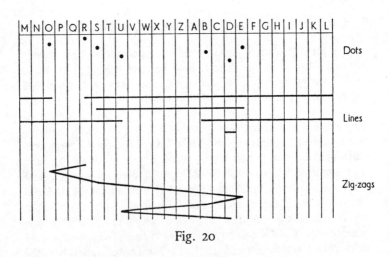

Fig. 20

The analysis of the mail could be a very lengthy process and, in order to plug up as many channels of secret communication as possible, most Allied censorship stations banned in advance the sending of whole classes of objects or kinds of message. For example, letters containing moves in an international chess game. The chess board, after all, does resemble the latitude and longitude lines of a map and the pieces could be grouped to suggest naval positions. Newspaper crossword puzzles were similarly suspect, for similar reasons. There could be a message concealed in a clue or a pass-word in an answer. Newspaper cuttings were banned because there might be helpful information in the actual text, or an agent might have concealed a message by pricking various words with a pin. Also banned was anything to do with numbers. If a censor came across loose stamps they would be taken out and replaced. Three stamps with, say, denominations 2, 5 and 10 cents might spell out a code signal 2510, or the time for an attack, 10.25 am —anything. So denominations 2, 5 and 10—value 17 cents— would be replaced by stamps of equal worth but different face values, perhaps 4, 6 and 7 cents.

Lovers' tender kisses at the bottom of private letters were cruelly deleted or, if the censor had a soft heart, added to. It did not matter which, as long as the number of kisses was altered. Lists of school swimming records or Johnny's latest height and weight, anxiously awaited by doting grandparents, were ruthlessly cut out. The grandparents might be the German Navy or the German Army and Johnny the latest Allied submarine or fighter plane. Eliminated, too, were knitting patterns. The simple direction 'P into back of 2 : K into front on 1 and slip both' suddenly takes on sinister overtones if your mind is running on enemy submarines sinking Allied battleships. Some stations at the beginning of the war actually employed knitters to knit up sweaters to see if there was any message concealed in the Fair Isle pattern. But the procedure was dropped as too time-consuming.

Cables ordering flowers, letters in unusual languages, gramophone record requests sent to radio stations, were all banned. And drawings—which, however pretty, were also pretty suspect. A bridge, a river, a castle in the background (Fig. 21). Very nice, very rural—recalling for an absent friend overseas happier days before the war. But, in fact, concealing a dan-

Fig. 21

gerous message: 'Queen Mary due Rio March 14th 18 hundred hours.' A submarine, a well-placed torpedo, and a terrific military and propaganda coup for Germany as the giant *Queen Mary* settles on the bed of the south Atlantic. The message, in morse code, is in the blades of grass along the nearside river bank, and reads from left to right: long long short long (Q) short short long (U), short (E), short (E), long short (N). And so on.

All these methods are highly ingenious, but are useful only for short messages. It was the ordinary-looking letter that contained larger messages and made up the bulk of items censored. Because trained enemy agents never sent letters that looked or sounded suspicious, the censors on Bermuda always looked for letters that seemed to have no reason for their existence. Nadya Gardiner:

The more innocent a letter, the more suspect it was. If we got a business letter which didn't seem worth the postage we would look at it and if we felt that this was suspicious we would ask the financial people or the business people to look out for more mail going between the same two people and if we got a series of these letters which continued to say nothing and to progress nowhere, we'd feel pretty sure that we had something suspect.

Punctuation could be a give-away.

We had one which was written in English, emanated from what was supposed to be a Portuguese company, but after the greeting they put an exclamation mark, Dear Manuel! which no Portuguese would use, which is not used in English but which is typically German.

The censors found that the way people addressed envelopes is as distinctive as handwriting.

If they type the top line in capital letters, they do it in capitals each time. If they double space between the address and each line, they do that each time.

With well-trained visual memories, the censors were now able to pick out the letters from Joe K by just looking at the envelopes. And they soon discovered that the letters inside were written in 'open' or 'jargon' code.

Because the cipher is so cumbersome to use, most agents in World War II very soon switched to open code, that is to say, a communication which looks like a letter but in which there is a secondary meaning to practically everything that has been said.

The French Ambassador in Russia was already using this technique of double-talk in the eighteenth century, as in this letter to Paris about the state of the fur trade:

Fox is no longer very fashionable here in St. Petersburg. Wolf is all the rage but there is a steady sale for moleskins and I understand some 30,000 are soon to be despatched from a firm in London.

All French envoys were issued with a code-dictionary in which nations were referred to under the names of fur. 'Wolf' was Austria, 'Fox' was England, and 'moleskins' were English troops. With this information, the real meaning of the letter is quite apparent.

Joe K's method was almost identical, as in this letter to a Manuel Alonso in Madrid:

| *Apparent meaning* | *Real meaning* |
| --- | --- |
| Your order number 5 is rather large | You've asked me for rather a lot of information |
| and I, with my limited facilities and funds shall never be able to fulfil such an immense order completely | and I haven't enough agents or money to be able to supply all the information you want |
| but I have already many numbers in stock and shall ship whatever and whenever I can. | but I've already got some of the information and will send it whenever I'm able to. |

Other letters went to Portugal. Close scrutiny by British agents in Lisbon showed that the postal addresses were back-door entrances to the German Embassy. Manuel Alonso was merely a cover-name for the German secret service.

Once we knew the letters were positive enemy messages and we'd held them up too long to send them on, we worked on them, analysed them, phrase by phrase, piece by piece, made copies, shuffled them together to try and get everything with the same references in the same stack. And then we realised these long chatty letters contained a lot of information.

On the backs of Joe's envelopes were return addresses in the United States. Investigation showed them all to be fictitious. Apart from the New York post mark, there were no other clues to Joe's identity and no possible hope of tracking him down. Miss Gardiner had to look elsewhere.

I sent the letters up to the lab. and asked them to be checked for secret writing. I received perpetually negative reports and yet I was convinced that they had this something on them, that there was an ulterior meaning—that I just about drove the labs. crazy. And they said, 'well, you're not a scientist, we're the technical people, we've tried every damn thing, there's nothing on these letters.' And I said, 'well, for God's sake, have you tried iodine vapour?' And they said, 'well, that's old-fashioned.' I said, 'well, try it.' They did, and there it was, secret writing.

Invisible writing is as old as the ancient Greeks. Milk, fruit juices, vinegar, even urine can be gently warmed into visibility. And, despite their age and the small protection they give, those methods are so convenient that they were still used in World War II.

Colourless chemical solutions are a more modern invention. Ferrous sulphate will be visible only when painted over with potassium cyanate, which turns the invisible writing bright orange. Copper sulphate solution becomes visible only when the writing is exposed to ammonia fumes. Clumsy spies, of course, give the game away by wetting the paper too much and buckling it, or by causing a tell-tale rough patch by pressing too hard and disturbing the fibres.

Censorship stations all had standard tests for invisible writing. Suspect letters were 'striped'. Three brushes, wired together to look like Britannia's trident, were dipped in different secret ink developers and drawn diagonally across the back of a letter. If any of the developers caused a reaction, the whole letter could then be tested. If it did not, then further tests could be applied.

We noticed that a number of letters would have the date in Roman numerals (X.I.XIL) and others in Arabic numerals (10. 1.41). So we tried to discover what this might mean, and eventually we found out by comparing the variables that one set of numerals contained messages in one specific secret ink and the other one in a different specific ink.

To gain the advantage in the secret ink war it was essential to provide a constant supply of new inks faster than your enemy could discover new developers.

The test that Nadya Gardiner insisted the Bermuda lab try was a very simple one. They took a letter from Joe K and put it inside a grass-covered tray spread with iodine crystals. Within seconds the iodine vapour brought out the hidden message. Fully developed, it read: 'British have seventy thousand men on Iceland. The SS *Ville de Liège* was sunk about April 14th.' Miss Gardiner was correct. Joe was passing on valuable information. The ink Joe was using was a solution of pyramidon, a tablet readily available from chemists and used as a headache cure. At some time it must have cured more than a headache, as pyramidon is now on the British poisons list. What Joe had done was to crush the tablets, dissolve the powder in a little water and write on the paper with a toothpick—so simple a device that, had it not been for an alert censor, the labs would never have found it.

As with all codebreaks, the break is valueless if the enemy knows it has been made. Having discovered Joe's secret ink, the labs photographed the message and then returned the letter to its original state before sending it on to Europe. To cover their tracks the censorship labs always kept a stock of chemical reagents that made the inks invisible again without damaging the writing paper. Special gums were prepared to re-seal envelopes with the original type of glue and to re-stick stamps that had been removed in search of a concealed message. These precautions were necessary, as the German labs were most careful to check whether a different glue on an envelope indicated enemy investigation. Later on it frequently proved unnecessary to open envelopes at all. With nearly all sealed letters the glue never sticks near the top of the envelope. There is always a small gap. Two strong but slender wires can be inserted here and placed round the page of the letter inside, enabling the censor to wind the letter page tightly round the wires and extract it through the narrow gap in the envelope. The reverse process returns the page, and no one is any the wiser.

Joe's letters continued to be intercepted, read, photographed and sent on again—with the censor's mark prominently on the envelope. The mark was to convince the Germans that the letter had been read but not understood.

The importance of Joe's secret information was increasing every week. His network was obviously expanding and becoming more efficient. Now was the time for British Intelligence to pounce, and break the ring. But there was still no personal information in the letters that could help with Joe's identity. The only clue was the constant postmark—New York. But there were over ten million people in New York.

Then one day we had a letter come through which contained a rather hysterical message about an accident having happened to someone in Times Square.

The letter was addressed to Madrid, and, in the smudgy secret-ink message on the back, was the news that at the height of the New York rush hour Joe's friend 'Phil' had been knocked down and killed. His body had been taken to St Vincent's Hospital.

It was the break Bermuda had been waiting for. British Intelligence went to New York and, with the help of the American FBI, the identification of the dead Phil led to the identification of Joe himself. His real name was Karl Frederick Ludwig, and he was an American, brought up in Germany. He had become a Nazi in the early 1930s and had returned to the US and set up as a salesman in leather goods. It was his business letters dealing with leather sales that had provided his linguistic cover as a secret agent.

Joe was not arrested at once. He was carefully followed till all nine members of his ring were identified. Then the police moved in. Joe took fright. He made a bolt for the west coast and a boat for Japan. Trailed to Seattle by the FBI, he was arrested in possession of large quantities of pyramidon and bundles of toothpicks. He claimed he suffered from terrible migraine and always picked his teeth after meals. Joe got twenty years, and his arrest put a stop to a spy ring that could have done incalculable damage both to the British and to the Americans.

At the end of the war, when German secret sources became available, it was learnt that there had been only one group of correspondence going between New York and Europe that Bermuda had not detected. The station had been an incredible 95 per cent successful.

# 10     Operation North Pole

In Europe itself, the hot war, begun when Germany invaded Poland in September 1939, was followed by the phoney war— a strange eight-month period of quiet. Then Hitler struck. In quick succession Denmark, Norway, Belgium and Holland fell.

Opposition to the Germans was crushed on the surface but never crushed underground. The fight was continued by the national resistance movements and, in Holland especially, it was a struggle in which ciphers played a decisive part. It was a struggle, too, that was to influence the outcome of the whole war in Europe.

To help resistance movements, Britain established SOE, the Special Operations Executive in London. Secret radio links were set up between SOE and the occupied countries in order to keep the underground supplied with men, money and vital information. In return, SOE got equally vital information about the plans and intentions of the German enemy.

The men who defied the Germans in order to keep the underground ends of the radio link open were the secret agents. Parachuted into their own countries with forged papers and radio transmitters, they were known only by their code-names. 'Cabbage' was dropped in Holland, late in 1941. His first job was to contact London:

It wasn't easy. The Germans were everywhere and we had to carry our radio sets in suitcases. This was a great mistake because the suitcases were standard issue in London and all looked the same and the Germans soon got to recognise them. Many of our chaps were stopped in the street and caught. And hulking a heavy suitcase from place to place in wartime makes you pretty conspicuous, anyway. We had help from our girlfriends, but the suitcases were even heavier for them. We were all very green and inexperienced—both headquarters and ourselves.

In order to operate at all we had to find a safe house where we could transmit undisturbed. This wasn't easy either. Penalties for harbouring spies were death or transportation so the people living in the house were sitting on dynamite. They hadn't a hope in hell if they were caught. And then, after two days transmitting, so the Germans wouldn't hear us and track us down, we had to move. Which meant hulking the suitcase and the whole thing would begin all over again.

German counter-espionage were constantly on the listen. They knew that there were illegal radio transmitters operating all over the country and it was these transmitters that they hoped to turn to their advantage. They would do this by catching an agent whilst he was operating and 'reverse' the station. In other words, operate the transmitter so that London would believe it was still in Dutch hands. If the Germans could do this, they could do two other things—infiltrate and destroy the Dutch Underground and, more important, learn from London the date of the Allied invasion of Europe—and be prepared when it came.

The German Abwehr had its HQ in a middle-class suburb of The Hague. In charge was Major Herman Giskes. In January 1942, a Dutch informer told Giskes that he knew the date and location of the next parachute drop of radio equipment from England. Giskes did not believe him and told him to run to the North Pole. However, a few days later, the German radio intercept stations confirmed the informer's story when they reported a new transmitter operating somewhere near the Dutch capital. It was the opportunity for a 'reverse' that Giskes had been waiting for. As a joke against himself he called the operation 'North Pole'.

First, he had to track down the location of the transmitter. He did this by direction-finding. Four listening stations were placed in cars, spread out over an area of a hundred miles. When the transmitter went on air, the aerials in the listening cars were turned in the direction of the transmitter's sound. The angle at which the sound was clearest indicated the direction in which the transmitter was located, and the cars, with their aerials constantly turning, slowly converged on the secret agent. The operation took several days; the agent certainly moved, but eventually the direction-finders arrived at the town, at the street, at the very house in which the agent was operating.

It was Friday, 6 March 1942, and the house was in the Fahrenheitstraat in The Hague, only a mile from the Abwehr headquarters. Giskes gave the order to pounce. His officers waited in a side street till they heard the tell-tale click of the operator going on air; smashed down the house door and captured a young army officer called Hubertus Lauwers.

Lauwers' transmissions to London were, of course, all in special cipher. Giskes, during interrogation, tricked him into revealing it. It was called a double-transposition and was extremely long and complicated. For example, consider a typical Dutch underground message sent to SOE: 'Need more supplies by sixth December Stop Send advice Driebergen and Putten Stop Ends.' (Driebergen and Putten are small towns in Holland.) The cipher is worked on squared paper. The message is written across the page, one letter per square, starting in any column (Fig. 22). The columns are numbered in a pre-arranged order and the square is completed with nulls. The result is

```
                              N  E  E
      D  M  O  R  E  S  U  P  P  L  I  E
      S  B  Y  S  I  X  T  H  D  E  C  E
      M  B  E  R  S  T  O  P  S  E  N  D
      A  D  V  I  C  E  D  R  I  E  B  E
      R  G  E  N  A  N  D  P  U  T  T  E
      N  S  T  O  P  E  N  D  S
```

Fig. 22

```
   5   1  10   4   9   8   2   7  11   6   3  12
   c   h   g   h   c   r   g   t   h   N   E   E
   D   M   O   R   E   S   U   P   P   L   I   E
   S   B   Y   S   I   X   T   H   D   E   C   E
   M   B   E   R   S   T   O   P   S   E   N   D
   A   D   V   I   C   E   D   R   I   E   B   E
   R   G   E   N   A   N   D   P   U   T   T   E
   N   S   T   O   P   E   N   D   S   c   g   s
   h   m   c   g
```

Fig. 23

```
   5   1  10   4   9   8   2   7  11   6   3  12
   h   M   B   B   D   G   S   m   g   U   T   O
   D   D   N   E   I   C   N   B   T   g   h   R
   S   R   I   N   O   g   c   D   S   M   A   R
   N   h   N   L   E   E   E   T   c   t   P   H
   P   R   P   D   r   S   X   T   E   N   E   c
   E   I   S   C   A   P   g   O   Y   E   V   E
   T   c   h   P   D   S   I   U   S   E   E   E
   D   E   E   s
```

Fig. 24

shown in Fig. 23. Lauwers used a lot of c's, g's and h's as nulls. This was deliberate on his part, as we shall see later, and completed stage 1 of his ciphering up process.

In stage 2, another piece of paper is squared and numbered in exactly the same way. But this time the squares are filled up so that the message becomes completely jumbled. Lauwers took his column 1—h M B B D G S m—and wrote it across the page. He did the same with column 2, continuing across the page till the whole message had been transposed. It ended up as shown in Fig. 24. This completes the first transposition.

Stage 3 consists of rearranging the letters yet again to make the second transposition—this time in five-letter groups ready for transmission. Lauwers got the letters by once more reading down the columns in column order. So the first five letters are, from column 1, MDRhR. The second group is IcE (the remainder of the first column) and SN (the first letters of column 2). And so on to the end:

| | | | | |
|---|---|---|---|---|
| MDRhR | IcESN | cEXgI | ThAPE | VEBEN |
| LDCPs | hDSNP | ETDUg | MtNEE | mBDTT |
| OUGCg | ESPSD | IOErA | DBNIN | PShEg |
| TScEY | SORRH | cEE | | |

The letters and nulls of the original message are so mixed up as to make no sense at all. Lauwers was now ready to start tapping out his message in morse.

The trouble with a cipher like this was that it was so complicated that it was easy to make mistakes, both in enciphering and transmission. More important, all the squared paper business broke the spy's major rule—*never* put anything on paper.

Giskes, with Lauwers' cipher, felt that he was over half-way to successfully reversing the station, and could now broadcast as if he was the agent himself. But Lauwers was not too

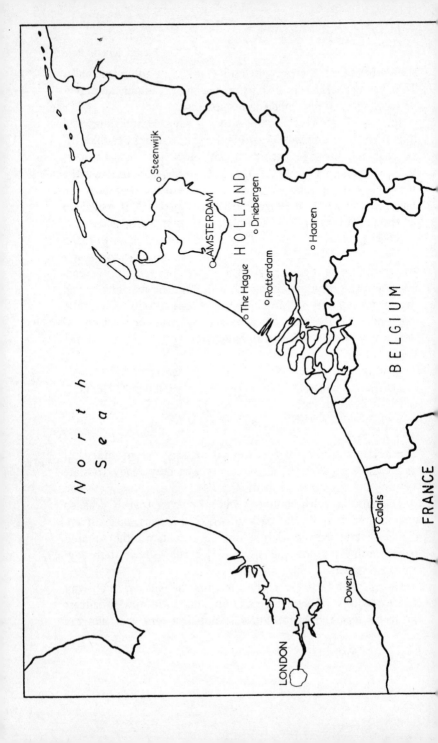

worried at having revealed his cipher as he had not revealed the security check. This was a pre-arranged coding mistake, incorporated in all transmissions, to tell London that the agent's message was genuine. Lauwers' security check was simple. He had to make a deliberate spelling mistake in the sixteenth letter of his original message. In the Driebergen-Putten message above, for example, the sixteenth letter was S. This Lauwers would change to an X or a T. Without that simple check, London would know the message was phoney and that the agent had fallen into German hands.

Lauwers' chance to warn London came two weeks after his capture when Giskes made him send a message to SOE asking for more supplies. Giskes made Lauwers operate for the Germans because every radio operator has a distinctive fist, a way of transmitting as individual as the touch of a pianist, and if anybody other than Lauwers had operated the transmitter, London would have known. The message that Lauwers sent ended with the request that the supplies be dropped on Steenwijk Moor, a flat, sandy heathland close to a thick forest. The message also, unknown to the Germans, omitted Lauwers' security check. Two days after receiving Lauwers' message, London broadcast the signal for the drop to take place. Had London recognised the warning?

To mark the dropping spot from the air, Giskes placed the usual triangle of red and white lights in the heather. As night fell, he huddled in the shelter of a sand-dune and waited for the expected aeroplane. It came just after midnight and dropped five containers. As they floated to the ground, Giskes was still not sure whether he had successfully reversed the station. He could have been double-crossed. The containers might explode. But when they did not, Giskes had the proof he had asked for. London was not suspicious.

But why? What had happened to the security check? The answer is one of the biggest and most tragic security bungles of the whole war. The agents' transmitters, despite their large suitcases, were low-powered and gave a weak signal. Bad atmospherics and German jamming often meant that messages arrived garbled. But even when transmissions were clear and the security checks quite obviously missing, London still accepted the messages as genuine. SOE ignored the whole complex system it had set up to prevent the very thing that had happened—a reversed station.

Because of this, Giskes slowly infiltrated the whole Dutch underground. A station reversed meant an agent caught and members of the underground killed. At the height of the operation Giskes had fourteen reversed stations—all beaming false information to London, with London's replies going straight to Hitler himself. It was a classic case of one half of the London organisation not knowing what the other half was doing. As fast as London was ignoring the absence of security checks, the new agents it was sending to Holland were having the importance of security checks drummed into them. One of these agents was a young naval lieutenant, Pieter Dourlein.

I was dropped at night in March 1943. For the dropping operations I had a code name 'Paul'. As soon as I was on the ground I heard people calling 'Paul', 'Paul' and flashing lights. I thought they were my own people sent to meet me so I pocketed my pistol and went with them to their leader. And there I was arrested.

They took me to Driebergen for interrogation and I realised the Germans knew much more about the organisation than I did. They seemed to know everything. They even asked me for my security check. I eventually told them my code and a false check. They seemed satisfied and carted me off to the Gestapo prison.

With information like this Giskes was able to keep his captured stations running very smoothly and went to extraordinary lengths to keep it that way. He even sabotaged a German barge in Rotterdam harbour and then reported it to London as a great resistance coup. London was suitably impressed and continued to drop men and supplies into enemy hands.

Lauwers, meanwhile, still being forced to operate for Giskes, was sick with apprehension. He had been transmitting for seven months without his security check. He realised something was wrong and changed his tactics. He signalled to London, in open language, the message CAUGHT CAUGHT CAUGHT. How Lauwers contrived to send his mesage ranks amongst the most brilliant and inventive coups in the whole history of cryptography. The careful selection of his nulls was about to pay off.

The first groups of his transmitted message had been: MDRHR IcESN cEXgI ThAPE VEBEN. The vital letters were the third group and the first letter of group four, cEXgIT, and their morse equivalents:

| c | E | X | g | I | T |
|---|---|---|---|---|---|
| — · — · | · | — · · — | — · | · · | — |

By deliberately making an error in the morse transmission, Lauwers was able to shift the dash on the front of letter X to the end of the dot of E to give him . — (A) and . . — (U). He added two extra dots to the letter I to make H and there was his new message CAUGHT.

| Code group: | c | E | X | g | I | T |
|---|---|---|---|---|---|---|
| Original transmission: | — · — · | · | — · · — | — · | · · | — |
| Doctored transmission: | — · — · | · — | · · — | — · | · · · · | — |
| Final plain-text message: | C | A | U | G | H | T |

If Lauwers had not selected his nulls carefully in the first place, the deception would not have been possible. And he had to do it entirely in his head with a German standing over him with a gun. Lauwers signalled his mistake to London three times. Predictably, London, which did not spot the absence of security checks, did not spot this either. Lauwers' effort was wasted.

Pieter Dourlein was imprisoned at Haaren. It had been a monastery and the converted monastic cells overlooked an inner courtyard. Dourlein was placed in maximum security on the top floor. The cell was tiny, and the only light came from a small ventilator in the bricked-up window. All he could see from this peephole was the guard, permanently on duty, in the courtyard below. Dourlein, as aware as Lauwers that something had gone seriously wrong, planned to send his own warning to London. He made contact with the prisoners on the ground floor by tapping morse on the hot water pipes. He got a safe reply and entrusted them with his message: 'All agents in enemy hands and prisoners at Haaren'.

Somehow, the message actually got to England where it was read by the officers in the London HQ. These men still firmly believed that all was well with their radio agents in the Dutch Underground. And, after careful consideration, they made their pronouncement. Dourlein's message was a deliberate fake sent by the Gestapo. It was to be ignored.

Dourlein, unaware, of course, of the fate of his warning, was worried that he had been unable to give London sufficient information. So he planned to escape.

I wanted to get out to prevent the Germans doing further damage, maybe getting hold of really vital information. I realised I had to risk everything to prevent that. I also realised that as soon as the Germans had finished with us they would shoot us anyway.

In the courtyard was a sentry with a searchlight and machine gun. At night he would play the searchlight over the windows. So we couldn't get out on the outside, we had to get out on the inside. We climbed through the fanlight above the door into the corridor. Ran down the corridor into the lavatory where the window was situated outside the inner courtyard. We had ropes prepared to lower ourselves from the window, onto a small roof and then down into the grounds out of sight. From there we had to climb over a barbed wire fence which was about ten feet high. Outside that fence were sentries posted 200 yards apart. At every post were more searchlights, dogs and machine guns. If it hadn't been for lots of trees we'd never have got away.

Dourlein makes it sound so easy but, in fact, it was fraught with danger and one false move would have meant instant death. Immediately he had gone there was a general alert for his arrest. Giskes knew that if just one agent got back to London, it would mean the end of North Pole. The search for Dourlein went on for weeks over the whole of the Netherlands. But the one place the Germans did not look was Haaren. For several days, till the hue and cry was over, Dourlein lay low in a convent only two miles from the prison itself.

His subsequent journeyings took him three long months through occupied Belgium and France, into Spain and then to Gibraltar where he got a boat for England. When it docked, Dourlein was at last able to give his incredible information to SOE. He was met by officers of MI5 and taken away to be interviewed. The officers were very correct.

I got suspicious that they didn't trust me somehow. And when they interviewed me again and I told them all I knew, they said openly that they didn't believe me. They believed I was a double agent working for the Germans. After going through all I'd been through I didn't expect big brass bands or flags but I did expect a decent welcome.

Instead, Pieter Dourlein was put in gaol. London had ignored the missing security checks, ignored Lauwers 'caught' message, ignored Dourlein's smuggled message and now, face to face with the living evidence, ignored that as well.

But with such an accumulation of evidence, even London grew suspicious. No more important information was relayed to the underground and Giskes realised the game was up. On 1 April 1944, all North Pole stations in German hands broadcast the following message to SOE.

We understand that you have been endeavouring for some time to do business in Holland without our assistance. We regret this the more since we have acted for so long as your sole representatives in this country, to our mutual satisfaction. Nevertheless, we can assure you that, should you be thinking of paying us a visit on the Continent on any extensive scale, we shall give your emissaries the same attention as we have hitherto, and a similarly warm welcome. Hoping to see you.

Operation North Pole came to an end nearly two years after it had begun—the longest effective 'reverse' in history. During that time the Germans had received 95 parachute drops from England and collected 30,000 lb of explosives, 2,000 hand grenades, 3,000 sten guns, 5,000 revolvers, 500,000 cartridges, and 75 radio transmitters. They also collected a small bank of half a million Dutch guilders.

The Germans, luckily for the Allies, failed to discover the exact date of the Allied invasion, but they kept Holland a secure German bastion long after the rest of Europe had been liberated. But the real cost of North Pole was in men's lives. Of the 52 agents parachuted into Holland, 47 of them, as Dourlein expected, were shot. In the whole Dutch underground movement 1,200 people lost their lives. Responsibility for the debacle lay somewhere in London.

# 11     *The Purple Machine*

December 7th, 1941. A date which will live in infamy. The
United States of America was suddenly and deliberately attacked
by the naval and air forces of the Empire of Japan.

President Roosevelt, speaking to a packed Congress in Washington, the day after the Japanese raid on Pearl Harbor. The
entry of the United States into World War II started the long
haul to Allied victory four years later. But the historical
importance of the event has overshadowed the importance of
the secret intelligence activity that preceded it, and almost
prevented it.

The Americans have had a long involvement with codes and
ciphers, but it was not until 1917, when the Americans entered
World War I, that they set up their own Black Chamber—
similar to those already established in Europe. The man in
charge was Herbert Yardley. Between 1917 and 1929, he
claimed to have solved nearly 50,000 diplomatic telegrams
involving the codes of twenty different countries, but probably his greatest success came in 1922, the year of the
Washington Naval Conference.

The conference was called in an attempt by the United
States to limit Asian sea power in the Pacific Ocean. The
Japanese delegates were given very detailed instructions by

Tokyo on how to proceed. They were told the maximum power they were to try for and the minimum they should settle for. Obviously, the minimum deal was a very close-kept secret. But not to Yardley's Black Chamber, who had broken the Japanese diplomatic ciphers and allowed the US Government to know what the Japanese would settle for before the Japanese had even begun to negotiate. It was easy enough for the US to impose on Japan a humiliating treaty that left it very subservient, both to the United States and to Britain, who were allowed ten ships each in the Pacific to the Japanese six.

But Yardley's personal victory was short-lived. By 1924, certain members of the US Congress were raising the same kind of objections to secret intelligence work as had been aimed at Room 40 in 1914, and, finally, in 1929, the objectors won. The American Black Chamber was de-commissioned because 'gentlemen do not read each other's mail'. Shortly after he had lost his job, Yardley, one of the world's greatest cryptographers, wrote a book. In it, he revealed how the Americans, by decoding the Japanese messages in 1922, had been able to dupe the Japanese at the Washington Naval Conference. The Japanese, predictably, were furious. And the distrust they already felt for the United States turned into a hostility that renounced the naval treaties, expanded Imperial Japanese power in the Pacific and finally unleashed itself on America on that day of infamy in 1941.

The Pearl Harbor raid was not a sudden, impetuous gesture but the culmination of a series of well-laid Japanese war plans. As a cover for these plans, and to allay American fears, the Japanese Foreign Office despatched their ambassadors to Washington to talk about peace. From 1940 on, the Japanese were talking with two mouths—the diplomatic and the mili-tary—and the two of them never said the same thing. The American intelligence services, hurriedly regrouped in the thirties, kept a close ear on this Japanese offensive by picking up the Tokyo diplomatic cable traffic on the radio intercept stations that ringed the American coast.

The Japanese sent their messages in a code that was nick-named Purple by the Americans. They called it this because the first Japanese code, called Orange, had increased in diffi-culty and progressed through Red till it wound up as the most difficult—Purple. Purple was something new. It was not a pencil and paper code but one constructed on a machine.

Machine ciphers had been used for over a hundred years. The first of any importance was invented by America's first Secretary of State, Thomas Jefferson, as early as 1790. Jefferson took a spindle and placed on it twenty-five wooden discs. On each disc the twenty-six letters of the alphabet were written in jumbled order, so that the order on each disc was different (Fig. 25).

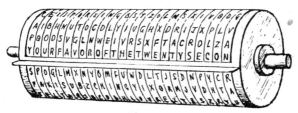

Fig. 25

Suppose [explained Jefferson] I have to cypher this phrase, 'Your favor of the 22nd is received.'

I turn the 1st wheel till the letter y presents itself.

I turn the 2nd and place its o by the side of the y of the first wheel.

I turn the 3rd and place its u by the side of the o of the second and so on till I have got all the words of the phrases arranged in one line. You will observe that the cylinder then presents 25 other lines of letters, not in any regular series but jumbled, &

without order or meaning. Copy any one of them in the letter to your correspondent. When he receives it, he takes his cylinder and arranges the wheels so as to present the same jumbled letters in the same order in one line. He then examines the other 25 lines and finds one of them presenting him these letters 'your favor of the 22nd is received', which he writes down. As the others will be jumbled & will have no meaning, he cannot mistake the true one intended.'

Jefferson had introduced a revolutionary idea into cryptography.

An Englishman, Sir Charles Wheatstone, displayed his cipher machine in 1867. It still exists, and consists of a dial with two alphabets and two clock hands, a long one and a short one, connected by gears. The long hand points to the outer (plain-text) alphabet, which includes a blank for a word space, and the short hand to the inner (cipher text) alphabet (Fig. 26).

Wheatstone provided operational instructions.

At the commencement [of encipherment], the long hand must correspond with the blank of the outer circle and the short hand be directly under it. The long hand must be brought successively to the letters of the despatch (outer circle) and the letters indicated on the inner circle by the short hand must be written down. At the termination of each word the long hand must be brought to the blank, and the letter indicated by the short hand also written down. By this arrangement, the cipher is continuous, no intimation being given of the separation of the words.

The only advantage that these relatively simple devices had over traditional ciphers was speed. And the greater the need for speed, the more the intelligence services experimented with machine ciphers, building on what Jefferson and Wheatstone had begun. In the 1920s and 30s, the Dutch, the Germans, the Americans and the Swedes had all produced, for commer-

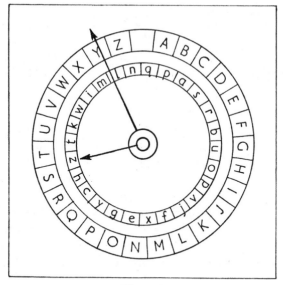

Fig. 26

cial sale, cipher machines that incorporated cipher wheels which, at their simplest, were operated by typewriter keyboards. The Japanese were among the nations who bought these machines and, with their traditional ability to develop and improve other people's inventions, came up with the Purple machine.

Purple, with the highest Japanese security classification, was used by their Foreign Office in only thirteen key embassies and consulates abroad—which included Washington and New York. The Americans, if they were to understand the secrets of the Japanese, had to break Purple.

The man given the job was William Friedman. His task was to reconstruct a machine he had never seen and which the Japanese believed impregnable. Apart from his own intelligence and experience, all he had to help him was previous

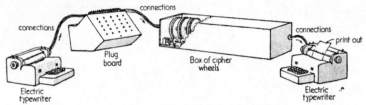

Fig. 27

work done on Red and a team of devoted analysts. It took a year and a half before Friedman produced something that resembled the Japanese original.

In essence, Purple consisted of two electric typewriters, separated by a plugboard and a box of cipher wheels (Fig 27). To encipher a message, the plain text was typed on one typewriter and the cipher text printed out on the other typewriter. It sounds easy, but this was by far and away the most sophisticated cipher machine yet invented, and, in its way, it has never been surpassed.

The Japanese alphabet consists of a mixture of over fifty letters and two thousand Chinese hieroglyphics: too much for an ordinary typewriter to cope with, so the Purple machine worked on Roman letters, A—Z.

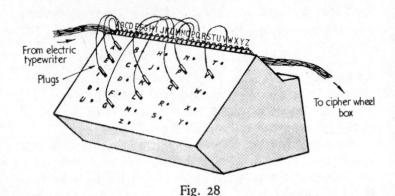

Fig. 28

The enciphering process starts on the left-hand typewriter. Each key on the typewriter keyboard has a wire linking it with the plugboard. The plugboard (Fig. 28) is like a telephone switchboard. It has twenty-six holes lettered A to Z and a wired plug in each of them. As electric impulses are received from pressing the typewriter keys they are re-routed and sent on to different destinations by rearranging the plugs in the plugboard. So if an O plug is placed in the hole marked G, the letter O pressed on the typewriter will be changed into a G by the plugboard. This is an encoding process in itself—a simple substitution, so simple that it is very easy to break. But the Japanese, according to a predetermined plan, switched their plugs around each day and confused the enemy by constantly ringing the changes on the plugboard alphabet.

But the real complications are still to come. The letter O, already changed into a G by the plugboard, travels along the G wire into the box containing the cipher discs—the most complicated part of the whole apparatus. The discs are slotted into the box like so many records in a record rack. Each disc (Fig. 29) represents a different letter, and, as in Jefferson's 1790 original, each disc has written round its edge the twenty-six letters of the alphabet in jumbled order.

The original O, now a G, after the plugboard travels to the disc standing in the G position. This may represent the letter S. If it does, the S is what

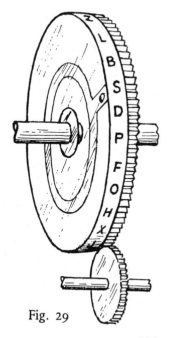

Fig. 29

will be printed by the second typewriter. But this must not happen twice and this is the real cleverness of the machine. A series of cogs is attached to every cipher wheel, and after the letter S has been typed the cogs turn the cipher wheels a number of spaces. This changes the path of all the electrical impulses. So, if O was typed three times running, it would come out as a different letter each time—firstly S, then perhaps T, then M. As a result of this constant interaction of all twenty-six cipher discs, it is possible that a single word can be coded in thousands of different ways.

To break a normal cipher it is necessary to do a frequency count—to count the number of repetitions—but Purple is so constructed as almost never to repeat itself, and a frequency count is useless. Remembering this, Friedman's achievement was quite incredible. Even to this day, some Japanese involved with Purple refuse to acknowledge that Purple was broken by Friedman at all. They believe that the machine was photographed by the Americans in the consulate in New York. Though there is some evidence for this, no one really knows or, if anyone does, he is not talking, and the most likely informed guess is that Friedman did, with some indirect espionage help, construct the machine almost from scratch.

With Purple in their possession, the Americans could decipher all Japanese diplomatic messages. And there were now plenty of them. In October 1941, the war party in Japan took over the government and put into operation their plan to attack Pearl Harbor. At Pearl Harbor itself was Captain Joseph Rochefort, head of the Intelligence:

> Though we didn't know it at the time, the Japanese envisaged a strike against the United States at Pearl Harbor by sending a large air group from the North Pacific and making a sudden strike against the American forces there for the purpose of eliminating them for a period of months.

In Washington, the Japanese ambassadors Nomura and Kurusu continued to present their proposals for a lasting peace. At the same time, sailing one by one so as not to attract American attention, thirty-two ships of the Japanese strike force slipped out of Japanese territorial waters. On board the ships were four hundred and thirty planes of the Japanese airforce. US Intelligence plotted the course of the vessels by intercepting their radio messages. Then, suddenly, the Japanese disappeared. Captain Rochefort guessed what had happened:

> In our analysis of the radio traffic we were normally in a position to say where the major parts of the Japanese Fleet were at almost any time. Like we'd say they're in the home ports, they're training or that sort of thing. I would say from about 1st December on, we'd lost our knowledge of their activities and their positions because they'd gone into radio silence. That is they were not using their radios. Primarily, I would say our feeling was one of apprehension engendered mostly by the fact that we didn't know where any of these people were.

In fact, the Japanese were already well on their way to Pearl Harbor, and on 2 December turned towards Pearl Harbor itself. The Americans there had taken only the most elementary anti-war precautions.

> At one point we seemed to have a sort of freezing of the mind, a mental paralysis because our reasoning went like this—that if the Japanese attacked Pearl Harbor then this means war—war with the United States is going to be won by the United States. So, therefore, why should the Japanese attack Pearl Harbor? And the answer is that they don't.

With naval intelligence nil, Friedman's Purple machine gave the only clue to Japanese intentions. In Tokyo, the government drafted its final ultimatum to Washington. The problem

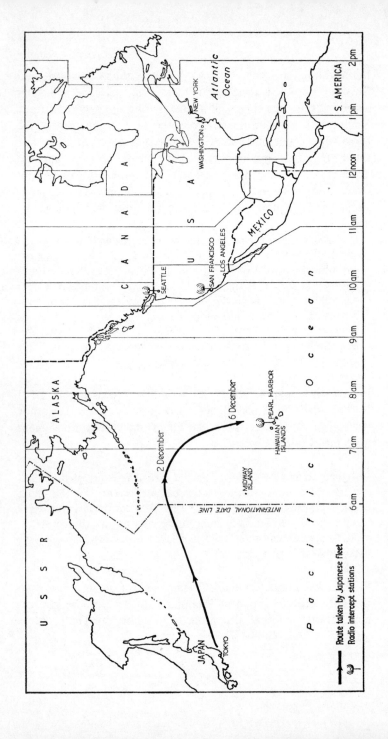

was when to send it. According to the Hague Convention, 'hostilities must not commence without previous and explicit warning'. The Japanese wanted to comply with international law whilst, at the same time, maintaining the maximum element of surprise in their attack on Pearl Harbor. They came up with an ingenious answer. Pearl Harbor time is six hours behind Washington time. So, if the Japanese hit Pearl Harbor at dawn, 7.30 am, it would be 1.30 pm in Washington. And if they delivered their ultimatum in Washington at 1.00 pm, it would give the Americans a mere thirty minutes to prepare for the attack—wherever the attack might come.

On 6 December 1941, the day before the attack was due, the Japanese began sending their ultimatum to their Washington Embassy. To ensure maximum security, they sent it in Purple and in fourteen separate parts over a period of eighteen hours. In the Japanese Embassy, the code-clerks began to decipher the messages. Scarcely a mile away, in the US Navy building, the Americans were doing the same.

In the early hours of 7 December, part fourteen finally arrived. De-coded, by the Americans, it read: 'The Japanese Government regrets, in view of the attitude of the American Government, it considers it impossible to reach an agreement through further negotiations.' This amounted to a declaration of war, but the message also included instructions to the Japanese ambassadors not to deliver it till a part fifteen arrived. This finally came at 7.30 am, Washington time, and the Americans noted that it told the ambassadors to deliver the ultimatum at 1.00 pm. The Navy cryptanalysts passed the information to the office of the Chief of Naval Operations, Admiral Stark, where it was delivered to a junior officer, Captain McCollum.

I was getting increasingly nervous. I stood in Admiral Stark's outer office and figured out the time differentials in various places where something was likely to happen. We wondered why the insistence on one o'clock.

It did not take them long to work it out. One o'clock Washington time was 7.00 in the morning at Pearl Harbor.

We fully expected war to take place at one o'clock Washington time. We didn't know Pearl Harbor was going to be attacked for sure, but we did expect war to start and Pearl was the most likely place.

The brilliant work of the American cryptanalysts who had decoded the Japanese text so quickly, combined with the Navy's analysis of the time differentials, enabled the US government to guess the Japanese intentions six hours before Japan was ready to attack. But the government did nothing.

Some people felt a warning should be sent to Pearl but the general feeling in Admiral Stark's office was that every step had been taken for this eventuality and all we could do was to wait and see the war come.

The Japanese fleet was now only 250 miles from Pearl Harbor and the planes it carried were well within striking distance of the target. The whole force was keyed up for action. Over the dark, still Pacific Ocean it was just beginning to grow light in the east. It was six am. In Washington it was already midday and the Japanese Embassy was in trouble. Ordered to dismantle their coding machines, the clerks were unable to decode Purple fast enough. They had decoded the short part fifteen, which told them when to deliver the ultimatum, but half of the long, vital fourteenth part, which contained the Tokyo ultimatum, was still unread. As a result, the ambassadors were forced to ask for a postponement of their one o'clock meeting with the US authorities.

But there was no postponement in the Pacific. Tokyo's attempts to synchronise their diplomatic and naval activities began to go wrong. The planes were prepared, the pilots briefed. Commander Mitsuo Fuchida, who was to lead the attack, ordered his men into the planes.

On the day of December 7th, thirty minutes before sunrise, we took off from the aircraft carriers and I was riding on the first plane leading the entire Japanese air squadron. Behind me three hundred planes were following. I was so proud. I felt a great responsibility for the whole Japanese nation for their destiny was dependent on the Pearl Harbor attack.

When the Japanese planes were actually in the air, the US Navy, having decided merely to sit back and see the war come, changed its mind and decided, after all, to send a warning to Pearl Harbor—just in case. It arrived as the first wave of Japanese planes was screaming round Diamond Head. Fuchida:

I saw the main force of the American Pacific Fleet were at anchor in the bay so I dispatched the first order 'Toh Toh Toh'—which was 'All squadrons into attack'. And the time was 7.49 in the morning. We dropped fifty bombs. One of them hit the battleship *Arizona*, and the magazine exploded. From that time the Pacific War had begun.

In Washington, the Japanese ambassadors delivered their ultimatum to the State Department over an hour late. They were met by tight-lipped silence. The first reports from Pearl Harbor were already coming in.

For the Japanese, the attack itself was a great success but, because their time schedule had misfired, they attacked America without warning and broke the Hague Convention. It was this international legal nicety that enabled the Americans to pin the blame for starting the war on the Japanese.

For the Americans themselves, Pearl Harbor was the greatest naval loss in their history. In the blazing ship *Arizona* alone, 1,200 men were entombed and died. Altogether they lost 2,500 men, 300 aeroplanes and 18 ships. But they need not have done. The men who broke Purple had provided the warning. It was the naval command who, for reasons of their own, decided not to act on it. In the history of cryptography, Pearl Harbor is the prime example of the codebreakers supplying the ammunition and the politicians not using it. It was to be two years before the politicians made amends, and the Americans got their revenge.

# 12　　　*Eyes in the Desert*

If you cannot break a code—steal it. Probably the most successful theft was by a little-known Italian called Loris Gherardi, and if he had failed in his mission there might never have been the legend of Rommel, the Desert Fox.

In North Africa, in World War II, the Germans were out-numbered by the British by three to one. But in the autumn of 1941 they were steadily advancing. The Americans, new to the war, watched the British retreat with considerable concern and it was the job of their military attaché in Cairo to liaise with the British and tell Washington exactly what was going on. The man who did the job was Colonel Fellers:

> I learned very soon after I got to Cairo that if I was going to be a good observer and write good reports I'd better report what I saw myself. Some people in Washington had the idea that the British were handing me all my material. That's an injustice to the British because they weren't but they permitted me to go wherever I wanted to go in the desert and it wasn't difficult to learn a great deal.

What Fellers learnt, he cabled to HQ in Washington, encoding his messages in a new and top secret code called Black—from the colour of its binding. Fellers probably guessed the enemy were monitoring his messages but, as Black was almost impregnable, they would remain secure. What he did not guess was that Black was already in enemy hands—stolen in September 1941 from the US Embassy in Rome. The man in charge of the operation was the head of Italian Military Intelligence, General Cesare Amé:

> The operation wasn't so difficult. All I had to do was reach for the American Embassy key from my office wall. Except for the Russian, I had the keys of all the foreign embassies in Rome. The operation itself was carried out by two specialist NCO's from the Carabinieri and two embassy staff—Italian spies working there as servants. One of them was Loris Gherardi, a man of about forty. Gherardi opened the embassy safe and noted exactly how the documents were placed. The Black Code was removed and rushed by car to be photographed in great detail at the Headquarters of the Italian Secret Service. Then, within hours, it was returned to its exact position in the embassy safe so that nobody suspected a thing.

The Italian Foreign Minister smugly noted in his diary: 'Everything that the US Ambassador telegraphs is now read in our decoding offices'. Also read were the messages sent by the other users of the Black code; in other words, almost the entire intelligence output of all the US embassies in Europe and North Africa, including, of course, Cairo.

The problem that faced the Italians was whether to hand the code over to their allies, the Germans. The uneasy alliance that existed on the battlefield existed, too, between Italian and German intelligence. Amé decided to keep the Black code to himself and give the Germans only the decodes. If the Germans wanted the code they would have to listen to Cairo direct and break it themselves, the hard way. Which is what they did.

In the small town of Lauf, near Nuremberg, the Germans had a radio intercept station that could pick up morse messages from anywhere in the world. Here they began to listen for Fellers in Cairo—occasionally intercepting messages and forwarding them to Berlin for decoding. The cryptanalysts in Berlin broke Black at the same time as Fellers began his detailed reports of British positions in North Africa. The Germans suddenly realised the staggering importance of what Fellers might say. Dr Herbert Schaedel was in charge at Lauf:

> They went crazy at Supreme Headquarters to get all the telegrams from Cairo. There were two that were of much importance. Two which always began either Milid. Wash. or Agwar Wash.—that was the abbreviation I think for Military Intelligence Division Washington and Adjutant General War Office Washington. And all these telegrams were signed with the name of Fellers.

As the messages always began Milid Wash or Agwar Wash, it was easy for the Germans to pick out, from the hundreds of coded messages going through Lauf each day, the important ones from Cairo. It also helped them decode the message in double-quick time.

Black was a fairly complicated two-part code. No one knows exactly what the code groups were as Black no longer exists, but it began something like this:

| | |
|---|---|
| Against | 28143 |
| AG War (Adjutant General War Office) | 19307 |
| Aircraft | 76140 |
| Airdrome | 34296 |
| Airplane | 54310 |

Encoded, a Cairo message would look like this:

| Plain text: | To AG War | British to withdraw | 270 |
|---|---|---|---|
| Code text: | 19307 | 59270 | 34975 | 10087 |

| | planes | from | combat | area |
|---|---|---|---|---|
| | 61924 | 77590 | 82134 | 55183 |

But these were not the code groups actually transmitted. Over a period of months, groups would be repeated, and, to avoid the code being broken by a simple frequency count, the code groups were re-enciphered. That meant that the Americans added another number to each group of the message, and the result of the addition was the group actually cabled to Washington. For example:

| Plain text: | To AG War | British to withdraw | 270 |
|---|---|---|---|
| Code groups: | 19307 | 59270 | 34975 | 10087 |
| Re-encipherment number: | 15000 | 15000 | 15000 | 15000 |
| Group transmitted: | 24307 | 64270 | 49975 | 25087 |

| | planes | from | combat | area |
|---|---|---|---|---|
| | 61924 | 77590 | 82134 | 55183 |
| | 15000 | 15000 | 15000 | 15000 |
| | 76924 | 82590 | 97134 | 60183 |

(Note that the addition is non-carrying: if a number adds up to ten or more, the ten is not carried into the next column.)

The original code group is now effectively disguised. The re-encipherment number changes each day according to a predetermined plan, and Black messages would go through with the same numbers rarely repeated.

Properly used, it is very effective. But the Americans made a mistake. They always began their routine messages in the same way—To AG War. The enemy knew this and simple arithmetic quickly revealed the code's daily disguise—the re-encipherment number. For example, the Germans receive the number 24307. They know that it is a cover for AG War and AG War is 19307. Subtract 19307 from 24307 and they have 15000—the re-encipherment number. Subtract 15000 from all the other transmitted code groups and there are the groups of the Black code itself. But the Germans could not have done this if Fellers had not always started his message in the same way. It took the Germans two hours to strip off the re-encipherment number, and decode and translate the message. Immediately, it was put into a German code and radioed direct to Rommel's intelligence unit in North Africa, 'where', as Dr Schaedel says, 'Rommel, each day at lunch, knew exactly where the Allied troops were standing the evening before'.

After their autumn advance the Germans had been slowly driven back again to Mersa Brega. Rommel, blind through lack of information, suddenly had one eye opened by Fellers' messages. His second eye was provided by his own intelligence unit. These men picked up local British messages and, according to General Westphal, Rommel's Chief of Staff, 'the British were very agreeable for us because they were quite broadminded in making speeches during the combat, and we had the possibility of making important conclusions from their speeches'.

The Germans now more than made up for their lack of numbers by superior intelligence and tactics. On 21 January 1942, with the help of intercepted information, they began to advance. In seventeen days they advanced an incredible three hundred miles and Fellers cabled Washington with the belief that Rommel would reach Cairo. To stop him, the British from their air base in Malta raided his African petrol supplies. The advance slowed. To get it going again, Rommel had to remove the air threat from Malta. Malta became a prime German military target. In two months it was battered by 9,000 tons of enemy

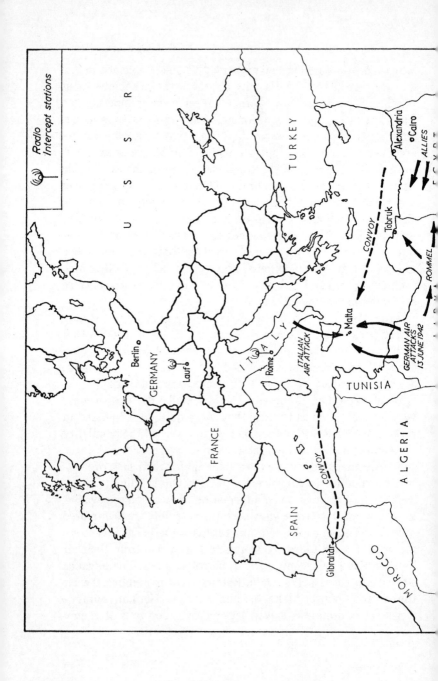

bombs, and by late May 1942 was so short of food and fuel that it was on the verge of surrender.

Malta was the key to Allied victory in Africa. It was vital that it should be relieved. Previous attempts had failed and the only possibility now was relief by Allied convoy. To minimise the effect of Axis air power, the convoy was split into two halves. One half was to sail from Gibraltar and the West; the other, from Alexandria and the East. Seventy-eight vessels in all. And, for success, only four ships needed to get through.

As the ships were prepared, Fellers, as usual, encoded his Black message for AG War in Washington. As the boats set sail, his message was intercepted by both the Italians in Rome and the Germans in Lauf. It read: 'Nights of June 12th, June 13th—British sabotage units plan simultaneous sticker bomb attacks against aircraft on nine Axis airdromes. Plans to reach objectives by parachutes and long range desert patrols. This method of attack offers tremendous possibility of destruction. Risk is slight compared with possible gains.' In other words, it was the British plan to safeguard the convoys by destroying the enemy planes whilst they were still on the ground.

On the night of 13 June the British paratroops went into action—and were picked up as soon as they landed. British bombers dropped their bombs on deserted airfields. The enemy planes had moved to safety, ready to blast the unsuspecting convoy on the following days. At first light both arms of the convoy came under heavy and continuous bombardment, the more devastating as it was unexpected. The enemy planes were joined by enemy submarines and enemy destroyers. Ship after ship was crippled or sunk, torpedoed or bombed. Three times the boats of the eastern arm had to return to Alexandria, the last time for good. But the Gibraltar convoy struggled on—to almost complete destruction. Only two ships arrived in Malta—enough food for a month and no fuel. 'In spite of our greatest efforts', said Churchill, 'the crisis in the island continued'.

Rommel's fuel supply stayed open. He continued his drive towards Cairo. Nothing, it seemed, could now stop him. But at this moment of supreme German success, things began to go wrong.

In a skirmish in the desert, Rommel's intelligence unit was overrun by the Australians. The loss of this experienced unit was irreplaceable. But worse was to come. After the Malta debacle, the British began looking for a security leak and in Rommel's captured papers was information that suggested the leak was coming from, of all people, the Americans. And the Americans meant—Fellers:

> The British came over possibly three months before I left Cairo in July of '42. And they wanted to see my security measures for the code. I showed it to them, and they seemed satisfied. They didn't say anything about the code being broken but it made me wonder why they were doing it.

The investigation of Fellers proved inconclusive, but British suspicions were confirmed in the most extraordinary way. In a piece of scripted propaganda on domestic German radio, the announcer made fun of the Americans by explaining the ease with which German intelligence picked up information from Cairo. The listening Allies could hardly believe it. The Black code was changed. And the enemy could no longer read a single word. Rommel was blind again. How German radio came to broadcast such a fantastic item has never been explained. Was it the work of a spy? Or an over-enthusiastic German patriot unaware of what he was giving away? No one knows. But whoever it was, he brought to an abrupt end the extraordinary leak begun by Loris Gherardi nearly a year before.

For Rommel, the leak had provided the clearest picture of enemy intentions ever available to a military commander.

Without it, it is doubtful whether he, the Desert Fox, the man always uncannily in the right place at the right time, would ever have gained his phenomenal reputation. But in the autumn of 1942, the tide of war turned against him. And the British advance began—perhaps coincidentally, perhaps not— as Fellers went off the air.

# 13 *Death in the Sky*

Despite Japan's initial success at Pearl Harbor, the Japanese Commander-in-Chief, Admiral Yamamoto, the man who had master-minded the attack, was worried. 'I fear', he said, 'all we have done is to awaken a sleeping giant and fill him with a terrible resolve'. Yamamoto was right. The Americans regrouped and within months began to push Japan back across the Pacific. In August 1942, the Americans poured ashore at Guadalcanal in the Japanese-held Solomon Islands. The Americans still had 4,000 miles to go to Tokyo, but at Guadalcanal they built Henderson Airfield. This was to be used as a jumping-off spot for further attacks on the Japanese still sitting a mere 400 miles away at the other end of the islands. And it was from here, too, that the Americans were to seek their revenge for Pearl Harbor on Admiral Yamamoto himself.

The extraordinary chain of events that led to Yamamoto's undoing began with Combat Intelligence Unit, the top secret codebreaking team the Americans had established at Pearl Harbor. This unit was assigned to work on the Japanese naval code JN 25—a code that incorporated some new and ingenious devices. Part of the encoding section is shown in Fig. 30.

The five-figure code groups are in jumbled order. The first four groups have opposite them, in Japanese and in alphabetical sequence, what each group stands for. Group 12951 is

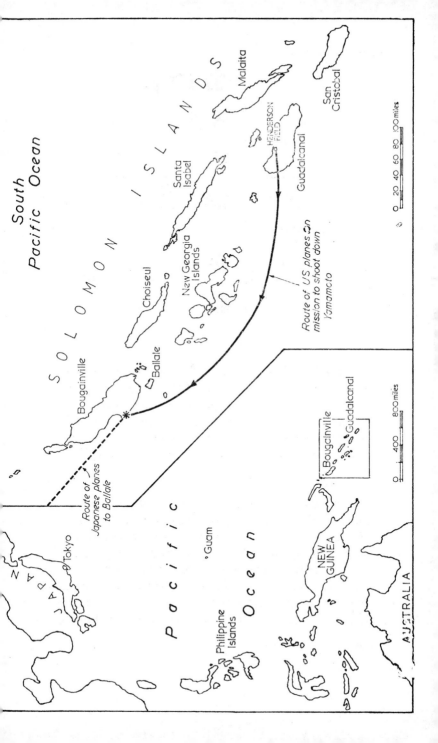

South
Pacific Ocean

SOLOMON ISLANDS

Malaita

San Cristobal

Santa Isabel

HENDERSON FIELD

Guadalcanal

Choiseul

New Georgia Islands

Route of US planes on mission to shoot down Yamamoto

0 20 40 60 80 100 miles

Bougainville

Ballale

Route of Japanese planes to Ballale

Tokyo

JAPAN

Guam

Philippine Islands

Pacific Ocean

NEW GUINEA

AUSTRALIA

Bougainville

Guadalcanal

0 400 800 miles

| 20463 | 咨 P,▶ |
| 40811 | 尒 F |
| 86660 | 尒 |
| 04069 | 寇荚辰空 |
| 12951 | |
| 44135 | GF |
| 58361 | 寇 |

Fig. 30

probably a null or an alternative group for the one immediately above it. But most significant is group 44135. In the column adjacent is not the group's meaning but another code group, GF—thus producing a code within a code, as GF stood for a particular geographical location. It was this unusual cryptographic combination that gave Combat Intelligence most trouble.

As well as GF, the code within a code included AK (Pearl Harbor), RA (Bougainville) and RKZ (Ballale). Combat Intelligence's problem was to make certain which letters referred to what locations. It was useless their breaking a message that said the enemy were about to attack AF if they were not sure whether AF was Midway Island or Pearl Harbor.

To make sure of the locations, Combat Intelligence used a well-worn cryptanalyst's trick. They sent out a message in an American code saying that Midway Island was running short of water. They knew the Japanese would break the code and read the message and, sure enough, three days later, the Japanese circulated the information to their fleet in the Pacific. The Americans picked up the message which said that AF was running short of water. Proof that AF was, in fact, Midway Island.

Another problem for Combat Intelligence was dealing with the enormous volume of Japanese traffic. The problem was made more difficult by the fact that there were fewer than a dozen people in the whole of the United States who had been cleared by security and who could also read Japanese. To make things easier, the unit installed, for the very first time, a punched card machine—rather like a very early computer. Every time a Japanese code group was recovered, both its Japanese symbol and its English meaning were written on a card and stored in the machine. Thus the machine became a bank of information. When a new Japanese message arrived, the machine broke all the groups it already knew, and left perhaps only half the message to be broken by the analysts.

On 29 January 1943, a New Zealand corvette, the *Kiwi*, made the work of Combat Intelligence very much easier. The corvette was cruising off Guadalcanal when it spotted a Japanese submarine, the *I–1*. In charge of the *Kiwi* was Commander Gordon Bridson.

It was nine o'clock at night. Almost dark. And the submarine, as soon as she saw us, dived out of sight. We attacked with depth charges and in the final stages could see her outlined by the phosphorescence of the water. We made two more depth charge attacks and then seemed to lose her. Several hours later we located her on the surface. We managed to get off three shots at her and she got off three shots at us. Finally she made the mistake of turning in front of us and crossing our bow. So I asked the chief engineer to give her all she'd got, and he says 'What for?' And I said 'In order to ram'. And he said, 'What do you do when you ram?' I said, 'I don't know, I've never done it before either.'

So he gave her all she had, and we hit her: rose right up on her. My immediate thought, sitting on top of the submarine was, 'What a bloody ridiculous place to be.' And to get off we had to go full speed astern.

In the morning all that was left of her was the bow sticking out of the water. And I'd no doubt in my own mind what were the results of our action. She'd clear gone.

But the result was more than the sinking of an enemy submarine; it was more significant than Bridson could possibly know, for on board the I–1 were twenty thousand codebooks of the new version of JN 25. Although the Japanese captain buried most of the codebooks in the sand on the sea-shore, the Japanese could not risk using a code that might already be in enemy hands. They were forced to bring into service a reserve version of JN 25 before it was really ready. It was in this simpler version of JN 25 that Combat Intelligence picked up a message that changed the whole course of the Pacific War. The analyst who worked on it was Alva Lasswell:

When you sense something's important you are spurred on. Normally, by two o'clock in the morning I might have gotten drowsy and fallen asleep but I had identified enough of the message to know that it was vital. I spent the rest of the night working on it, stretching my imagination to recover more and more of the code-groups till by morning I was sure enough to prepare a translation. I realised when I gave it to my commander that I was handing him a bombshell in this thing. That it would give him some uneasy moments in deciding how to use the information.

What the message revealed was that Admiral Yamamoto planned a one-day morale boosting tour of the Upper Solomon Islands. It gave details of his itinerary and showed that he was coming into the combat area for the first time. At 8.00 am on 18 April, escorted by six Zero fighters, he would fly to Ballale, in a 'Betty' bomber. The question was whether the Americans should attempt the impossible and try to shoot him down. There were moral as well as military objections. The US had never before attempted to murder an enemy leader—not even in war time. And if they did kill Yamamoto, there was always the danger that he would be replaced by someone more capable, more ruthless. The problem went to the President himself, then back to the Navy till it was finally decided that the elimination of the finest strategist in the enemy camp, the man who had planned Pearl Harbor, would rank as a major American victory.

At Henderson Field, a new plane, the P.38, could just about fly the 400 miles to make the intercept, but that was about all the Americans had going for them. Yamamoto was known to be punctual, but his exact route in the air would have to be guessed, his speed would depend on wind strength, he would be escorted by fighters and, with the American and Japanese flying at different heights, from different directions, for four hundred miles, the chance of actually making contact at 7.45 am was, to say the least, remote.

In charge of the operation was Captain John Mitchell :

We didn't think that we had the chance of a snowball in hell you know. But we had to go through the motions and we had to plan it as though we definitely would make the interception.

The Americans took off from Henderson at 6.25 in the morning, Mitchell leading, and behind him, Tom Lanphier, the man detailed to execute the kill. Seven hundred miles to the north and thirty-five minutes later, Yamamoto, the unsuspecting prey, took off for Ballale. Mitchell reached intercept point at 7.44 am.

I was about one minute early, according to my calculations. It was rather hazy that day and I was disturbed that I couldn't pick up the land—but once I did there were two Betty-type bombers. We were just practically on a collision course with them. We turned in parallel with the bombers and started climbing to get the right altitude. When I first saw them I called to Tom Lanphier. I said, 'There's your meat Tom. Don't miss him.'

Lanphier was now several hundred feet above the Japanese.

The lead bomber dived down and away. I wanted to get after this fellow but it was already apparent I couldn't get to him unless I did something about the three fighters coming up at me. I started firing long before I should have. I was frightened. I just started shooting with the machine gun. And this fellow's wing came off and he went under. And the other two fighters went on either side of me. So I flipped over and the bomber which had dived down was coming back and around, so I started down after him. It was already down on the tree tops, the one I was after—the lead one—and I was going too fast at the time to shoot him. So I started skidding around to slow up and in order to be sure my guns were working again I fired them, tested them. At the moment I tested them—I hit him.

If I'd waited till I was ready to shoot, I'd have missed him. But I fired this thing and his right engine started to burn and the bomber went down in the jungle; just plunged down in a big burst of flame.

Mitchell watched in amazement.

I had no doubt that we had actually shot down Admiral Yamamoto. I felt we had accomplished the mission. There was no doubt in my mind that he was—he was dead. And it was an act of God to have made this happen the way it did.

Not until four weeks later did Tokyo radio announce that Admiral Yamamoto, 'while directing general strategy on the front line in April this year, engaged in combat with the enemy and met gallant death in a war plane'. The nation was stunned. 'His loss', said his successor, 'is an insupportable blow to us'. And he was right. Japan never recovered.

# 14 *The Man Called Lucy*

The one embassy key that the Italian Secret Service did not possess in Rome was the Russian. This was not surprising, as the ruthlessly efficient Russians proved themselves probably the most successful spies and cryptologists of the entire war.

Cryptography came late to Russia, introduced from the West by Peter the Great in the early eighteenth century. During the nineteenth century the Tsars set up Black Chambers in every major Russian city and used them to track down any organisation that threatened their absolute rule. But the Chambers failed to save Tsar Alexander II in 1879, or Nicholas II in 1917, or to prevent the rout at Tannenberg in 1914. None the less, Russian intelligence methods were generally good, and, after the Revolution, they became even better when the Communists took over the Tsar's organisation and improved the original techniques.

In World War II this Russian organisation was put to severe test—and survived, brilliantly. A series of spy rings, tightly controlled from Moscow, operated in almost every country in the world, feeding back information vital to determine Soviet military and political strategy. Of these spy rings, three were particularly successful: the Red Orchestra, operating in Germany itself; the Sorge ring in Japan; and the Lucy ring in Switzerland, probably the greatest spy ring in World

War II. It was Lucy who almost certainly saved Russia from German defeat.

Switzerland, after the capitulation of France in 1940, became an island of freedom in occupied Europe. And an ideal base for the spy operations of all countries. The Russians were already well established. The Resident Director was a Hungarian map-maker called Sandor Rado—code-name 'Dora'. It is a Russian rule that the head of a network must never operate in the country he is spying against. Dora, spying against Germany, found neighbouring Switzerland a ready-made haven. He lived a respectable but rather secluded life, at the top of a block of flats near the centre of Geneva. From his balcony window he could see, a mere ten miles away, the mountains of occupied France. Dora, in classic espionage style, never met his agents in his flat, but always in the streets, in cafes or on park benches. It was here that he first met 'Packbo', a patriotic Swiss whose real name was Otto Punter.

> I was introduced to Dora by Carlo. And Carlo said, 'This is Packbo'. I knew only that he was a friend fighting fascism. Later I knew he was a Soviet agent but that was all. We didn't exchange names. Dora knew all about me but I had no address or 'phone number for him.

To protect both the embryonic network as a whole and themselves as individuals, members of the ring met infrequently and never knew the real identity of the person they were meeting. Dora and Packbo met in a small restaurant in the busy city centre, the Cafe Royale in the Rue du Mont Blanc.

> This restaurant had two entrances. We went in by different entrances and met inside. When we had information to exchange we carried newspapers with the information concealed between the pages. We would sit at the table, reading and chatting and drinking our coffee and then exchange the newspapers.

The information, mostly about industrial output in southern Germany, was usually written in milk on blank paper. It had to be warmed into visibility. Compared with James Bond, these rather primitive and stereotyped espionage methods seem laughable. But their simplicity is their strength. An agent, to be successful, must never draw attention to himself, and what more normal than newspapers and milk?

In early 1941, Dora expanded the ring again. He recruited 'Edward,' Edmund Hammel, the owner of a small radio shop in the Rue de Carrouges.

> I joined Rado's ring through Sonya who came to the shop to buy spare parts to make up transmitters. When Dora came to my shop he took every precaution before coming in. I kept a clock in the window. If it had stopped at midday he knew it was dangerous to come inside. If it showed the correct time then the coast was clear and he would go round through the side passage and up the back stairs to the apartment above the shop. Eventually I'd close the shop and join him there.

'Edward' became one of the network's radio links with Moscow, transmitting, not from the shop, but from his home on the city outskirts. The other radio link was established a few miles away in Lausanne by 'Jim'. Jim was the code-name for an Englishman called Alexander Foote. Recruited in London, he was specially sent by Moscow to join the Swiss net.

As the ring grew, so did the danger from the Swiss police and from German spies. Personal meetings in the Cafe Royale were no longer safe, and regular traffic of secret information passed through a 'cut-out'—that is, an anonymous messenger. If Packbo had information for Dora, he did not deliver it himself but put it in an envelope addressed only to 'M'. M, ignorant of Packbo's identity, collected the letter and took it to Dora. Thus, if Packbo was caught he could not reveal M's identity because he did not know it. And if M was caught, he knew neither Packbo's identity nor Dora's. So, whilst the police could catch an individual, they could not break the ring.

*Packbo*: A ring can only exist safely if only three people know each other. This was the error of the French Resistance. In the beginning everybody knew everybody else and if one of them was caught, all of them were caught. If you don't know the name of anybody you can't give them away to the police.

In the spring of 1941, Russia and Germany were still uneasy allies—but not for much longer. Just before Hitler declared war on the Soviet Union, the net was completed by Lucy himself.

Rudolf Roessler, operating from Lucerne—hence the code-name Lucy—has been called the greatest spy of the war. He was probably German, but left Germany for Switzerland when the Nazis came to power in 1933, and began working for the Swiss secret service. Very quickly he supplied them with remarkable information. He even told them the correct dates of the German invasions of Poland, Holland, Belgium and Denmark. The Swiss passed on the information to the Allies— but it was not believed, and Roessler, disappointed, began to work for the Russians.

*Packbo*: The information from Roessler was so fantastic and precise that it was really not easy to believe it.

*Edward*: To give you an example—when Hitler decided to attack Russia. Well, ten days before this happened, Dora came to me and said, 'I've a vital message which must go out this evening without fail because it says that Hitler will attack Russia in a week'.

Dora felt the message to be so important that he had broken the rules, ignored the cut-out, and taken the message to

Edward himself. But Stalin, like the Allies before him, refused to believe it. Which, in a way, was sensible, as Lucy refused to reveal his sources. For all the Soviets knew, Lucy might have been a double-agent feeding them false information. But when the Germans attacked as Lucy had predicted, Moscow was convinced that Lucy was genuine. From then on, the Swiss ring became the prime source of Moscow's secret information. Regular radio contact was made each night between Geneva/Lausanne and Moscow, and information passed in cipher.

The Russians encipher in English—always, because if the cipher is ever broken, it will not immediately be obvious that the messages are meant for Moscow.

The Lucy ring used a three-stage cipher. Although it was complex, it was economical and easily transmitted, as it recognised the fact that 60 per cent of the English language can be written using the eight letters A SIN TO ER. These letters are written out and numbered 0–7:

| 0 | 1 | 2 | 3 | 4 | 5 | 6 | 7 |
|---|---|---|---|---|---|---|---|
| A | S | I | N | T | O | E | R |

When these letters are used in a message they are enciphered with their single-number equivalents.

The remaining eighteen letters of the alphabet are written in sequence beneath the others and a square is completed by the addition of numbers eight and nine (Fig. 31). The two

|   | 0 | 1 | 2 | 3 | 4 | 5 | 6 | 7 | 8 | 9 |
|---|---|---|---|---|---|---|---|---|---|---|
|   | A | S | I | N | T | O | E | R |   |   |
| 8 | B | C | D | F | G | H | J | K | L | M |
| 9 | P | Q | U | V | W | X | Y | Z | . | / |

Fig. 31

additional symbols are a full stop and a spare which can be used for anything. These eighteen letters and the two symbols are each enciphered by two numbers. Thus, reading from the side and top, D becomes 82 and V becomes 93.

Now to encipher an actual message: 'Hitler to attack Russia'. First fill in the letters that have single-number equivalents:

```
H  I  T  L  E  R   T  O   A  T  T  A  C  K   R  U  S  S  I  A
2  4     6  7  4   5  0   4  4  0           7     1  1  2  0
```

The economy of the system is immediately apparent in that no fewer than fifteen of the twenty letters in the message can be enciphered by the A SIN TO ER groups. The rest of the letters in the message are enciphered with the double-figure groups:

```
H   I  T  L   E  R   T  O   A  T  T  A  C   K   R  U   S  S  I  A
85  2  4  88  6  7   4  5   0  4  4  0  81  87  7  92  1  1  2  0
```

So as to avoid the give-away of normal word spacings, the message is now collapsed into the usual five-figure groupings to give: 85248 86745 04408 18779 21120. This ends the first stage of encipherment.

The second stage involves a book of statistics. Any book will do, as long as it contains strings of figures—such as the number of beef cattle imported into Sweden in 1934, or the number of houses built in England in 1967. Open any page of the book at random, select a line, select a column, and start reading off the strings of figures; perhaps they will be: 3 1 3 4 5 8 6 0 9 2 3 5 2 9. These numbers are then added to the five-figure groups of the message:

| Original code groups: | 85248 | 86745 | 04408 | 18779 | 21120 |
| Random number from statistics book: | 31345 | 86092 | 35294 | 08435 | 76390 |
| Result of non-carrying addition: | 16583 | 62737 | 39692 | 16104 | 97410 |

The message is now unbreakable. The figures from the statistics book will never be used again, so a word will never be encoded in the same way. But, if it is unbreakable to an enemy it will be as unbreakable to the recipient unless he has a copy of the same statistics book and knows exactly where in the book the encoder started. This vital piece of information has to be included in the message itself and forms the third stage of the enciphering operation. The encoder, perhaps, started on line 11 in column 3 of page 71. This is written as a normal code group 11371 and then added to the fourth group of the message:

16104 + 11371 = 27475

The new code group 27475 is called the key group, as it is the one that will unlock the whole meaning of the message. Because of its importance it is buried in the message according to a carefully concealed plan known only to the recipient and sender. Perhaps it will come as the fifth transmitted group:

16583   62737   39692   16104   27475   97410

And there is 'Hitler to attack Russia' wrapped up in one of the most ingenious ciphers ever invented.

But there was a snag. A book of statistics may not be as big as the suitcase transmitters that the Dutch resistance lugged around, but it is still pretty bulky. Any suspected spy caught with a statistics book will have a lot of answering to do, so the Lucy ring soon switched to using ordinary books—

a pocket Shakespeare, a small Bible. The encoder, in the usual way, opens at random, page 99, line 15, starting third word in: 'hundred cubits, and the breadth fifty everywhere', etc. This happens to be from Exodus and is describing the measurements of holy garments. For enciphering purposes the letters of the sentences are merely turned into their figure equivalents on the basis of the alphabet, A to Z being numbered in reverse order 26 to 1. So, the word 'hundreds' becomes 19 6 13 23 9 22 23 8, and the figures are added to the code groups in the way described above. Similarly, the key group becomes (in the order: line, starting word, page) 15399. Even more ingenious. And with this cipher, the Lucy ring poured out a torrent of incredible information.

The German attack on the Soviet Union had taken the Russians completely by surprise, and within weeks the Germans had advanced six hundred miles, destroyed five Russian armies and taken a million prisoners. It was only the information from Lucy, beamed from Geneva to Moscow, that put the Russians back in the fight. So important and so detailed was the information, that Dora was having to encipher for twenty hours at a stretch. Exhausted and no longer able to cope alone, he once again broke regulations and farmed some of the material out to Packbo.

> I remember one cable in particular. It had the whole order of battle of Marshal Von Paulus before Stalingrad. There was the number of divisions, their commanders, the positions of each regiment; details right down to the number of guns. If I hadn't enciphered the message, I wouldn't have believed it. Even today. It was incredible.

By late 1942, the Lucy ring had been transmitting for two years. During that period both the Swiss police and the neighbouring Germans had intercepted hundreds of the network's transmissions. But they had failed to break the code. They did not know who was operating, or where the information was going. German agents, determined to find out, quietly crossed the border. The Swiss, to forestall them and preserve their own neutrality, decided to track the transmitters down themselves.

They did it very cleverly. Each district of the city of Geneva has its electricity supply from a central generating station. The police believed that the secret transmitter was operating on mains supply, so, if they cut the supply the transmitter would go dead. For the next few days each Geneva district in turn was treated to what the ordinary Swiss thought was a power cut. But when District F was cut and the transmitter went dead, the police knew exactly where to concentrate their search.

The following night they brought in direction-finders which led to the Route de Florrisant and a villa standing in its own grounds. As soon as it was dark, the house and grounds were surrounded by men, dogs and searchlights. It was essential to catch the operator in the act. At midnight, as the transmitter went on the air, the police pounced. The man they caught was 'Edward', Edmund Hammel:

> I guessed what was happening. I stopped trying to transmit and tried to put the machine and the papers away. But it was too late. The police smashed down the door and I was arrested.

In a hiding-place in the wall, the police found secret papers in Dora's handwriting. Although it was one of Moscow's golden rules never to have papers and transmitters in the same place, Rado, believing the Germans were on his tail, had panicked and removed all incriminating papers to Hammel's. It was these papers that the Swiss found—messages for transmission, both in cipher and in plain text, as well as the cover names of members of Rado's organisation—Packbo, Jim and Lucy.

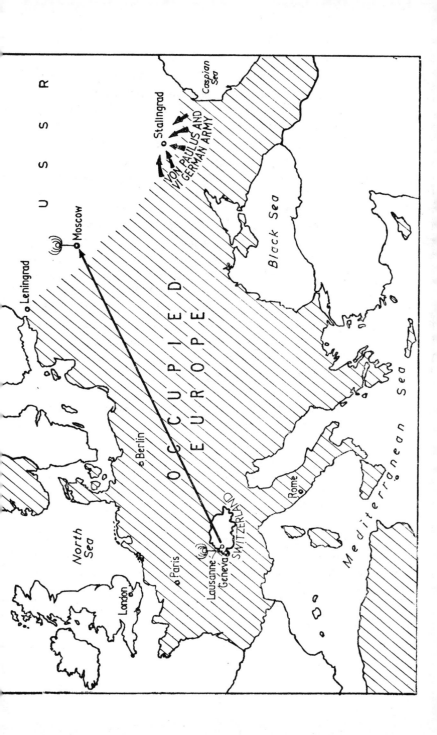

With the cipher now in their possession, the Swiss were able to learn the contents of previously intercepted messages and know that the messages were destined for Moscow. They also recognised that the cipher was very similar to another one used by a transmitter elsewhere in Switzerland.

With Edward already in police hands, Dora was forced to pass all his information through Jim, his other transmitter in Lausanne. Within a month, the police raided the flat and Jim was put in prison. Lucy soon followed him. Dora was on the run and the ring was at an end. But not its influence.

Four thousand miles away, Lucy's information about Marshal von Paulus' troops had enabled the Russians to halt the German advance at Stalingrad. For months, Paulus battered at the city but, thanks largely to the steady flow of strategic information from Lucy, the Russian lines held. Gradually, superior intelligence began to prove decisive and in late January the Russians split the German army in two. Paulus' Sixth Army was surrounded and forced to surrender. For the Russians, it was a military and psychological turning-point. It showed, for the first time, that the Germans could be beaten, and it started a German retreat that was to end only in Berlin and absolute defeat. As Packbo says:

> When Jim was arrested the war was practically decided. Lucy's information had been of the utmost importance in the battle of Stalingrad and I think that for the Wehrmacht, it was the beginning of the end.

That Russia fought the war on Lucy's information, is largely true. But where did the information come from? As it dealt with major tactics and reached Lucy within twenty-four hours of decisions being made, it must have leaked from very high up in Hitler's High Command. Perhaps Martin Bormann, Hitler's deputy? 'Impossible,' says Grand Admiral Doenitz,

Hitler's successor. 'Very unlikely,' says Albert Speer, Hitler's munitions minister. Then who?

The British? Stalin never believed a word Churchill told him, so it is just possible that Churchill fed vital information from the British secret service into the Russian net via Jim. Jim, Alexander Foote, was English and could have been a double agent. After the war he served with the Russians in Moscow and then defected in 1947 and was given a sinecure in the Ministry of Agriculture. Why? Foote complained about his British salary, but never revealed his secret—if there was a secret—and died in 1956.

Rudolph Roessler is also dead. He was convicted by the Swiss in 1953 for spying for Czechoslovakia, but steadfastly refused to talk about his life as 'Lucy'. Packbo, Otto Punter, is still alive, but never learnt the secret. Nor did Edward, Edmund Hammel, still running the same small radio shop in the same small street in Geneva. Nor, apparently, did Dora. Rado was made to pay for his mistakes. He spent fourteen years in a Russian concentration camp and resurfaced only in 1960—as Professor of Geography in Budapest. He has suggested that Lucy's information came from the Finnish Embassy in Berlin, or from a Leipzig lawyer with army friends, or was stolen from the Swiss secret service itself. So, all that we do know is that the head of the war's most successful ring—does not know. As Packbo says: 'Roessler took his secret to the grave and I think that it is best so'. What has survived him is a lot of speculation and a technique of enciphering that the Russian Intelligence Service has built on and used against the West to great advantage—as we shall see.

# 15                                          *D-Day*

By the beginning of 1944 the war in Europe was about to
turn in the Allies' favour. The Russians were advancing in
the east, and in the west the British and Americans were
about to launch 'Operation Overlord'—the code-name given
to the planned military landings on the French coast. The
whole D-Day operation was one of the best-kept secrets of
the war. The Germans had tried very hard to discover when
it was coming, through their Operation North Pole in Holland,
but they had failed. They knew it would take place but did
not know exactly when or where. Their Intelligence gave
top priority to finding out. Surprisingly, success or failure
was to depend ultimately on the intelligence security provided
by the British telephone and domestic radio.

The Germans, in 1944, were camped all along the Channel
coast. Hitler thought the attack would come in Normandy,
the rest of the High Command that it would come at Calais
—the shortest distance from England. Hitler was right; the
landings were planned for the beaches between Cherbourg
and Le Havre, but, fortunately, Hitler did not back his hunch.

To keep the Germans guessing, the Allies tried a number
of devices. They set up a network of phoney spies who fed
back false information to Berlin. They swamped the enemy
decoding bureaux with thousands of unintelligible messages in

peculiar ciphers. They launched 'Operation Fortitude' under General Patton—an entire fleet in Dover Harbour ready to sail to Calais at a moment's notice: except that the boats were all dummies. And they dropped a dead body in the Bay of Biscay, complete with false secret documents, which told the surprised Germans that D-Day was planned for the beaches of Spain. This way the Germans could never be sure which information was true and which was not. To be really sure, they had to get it from the horse's mouth—and the horse was Churchill.

Churchill conducted the war from the Cabinet Office, a warren of basement rooms buried under concrete opposite the Houses of Parliament. Linking the Cabinet Office with the important military and political centres in the outside world was a vast battery of telephones. To ensure secrecy, all telephone speech was scrambled. To make security doubly sure, the scrambling was done at source by the most efficient and effective scrambler machine yet invented. It was this formidable bunker and, in particular, this formidable machine, that German Intelligence had to penetrate.

Scramblers were almost as old as the telephone itself, but they had been seriously worked on only in the 1930s. The scramblers in the Churchill bunker were metal boxes about two feet square, kept on the floor beside the telephone. On the phone itself was a button. If the button was pressed ordinary telephone speech would be re-routed through the scrambler before being passed out of the building and into the ordinary telephone system.

Basically, the scrambler is a coding device. Just as a written message can be hidden under a disguise of letters or numbers, so a spoken message can be hidden under a distortion of sounds. There are a number of ways of doing this. Speech can be recorded at different speeds to produce the same effect as when an old 78 record is played at 33 speed and vice versa.

Or speech can be masked by covering the sounds of the human voice with additional noise to produce a meaningless sound blanket. But the simplest method is inversion.

The vocal chords of the human voice vibrate at different speeds. A high-pitched sound causes a fast vibration, a deep sound, a slow vibration. What the scrambler can do is to invert the sounds, so that a high-pitched noise comes out as a low one and a low noise as a high one. In practise it is a not very effective substitution where a=Z, b=Y, c=X, m=N, n=M and so on; an attuned ear can soon pick out the underlying message.

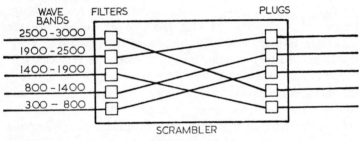

Fig. 32

More effective is band splitting, the method favoured by Churchill. In the normal way, the telephone converts human speech into a wave band which ranges from 300 to 3,000 cycles per second. Inside the scrambler, the wave band is split into five smaller bands ranging from 300 to 800, 800 to 1,400, and so on. These bands are then automatically re-assembled in jumbled order by shifting a range of contact plugs (Fig. 32). The result is a jumbled human voice which is quite unintelligible. The jumble can be varied merely by switching round the contact plugs. To descramble the message at the other end, the recipient has to arrange the plugs on his machine in the same way. This returns the sounds to the correct order and the message becomes intelligible again.

Churchill was a compulsive telephone user and, in his subterranean headquarters, had a hot line to President Roosevelt in Washington. Few people knew it existed because it was concealed in a room that guaranteed Churchill the utmost privacy. A small swivel catch on the outside said 'Engaged' and everyone thought it was the Prime Minister's personal lavatory, but inside there were just the phone, the scrambler and a clock that showed London and Washington time. Churchill, placing great faith in his scrambler, phoned Roosevelt about the most secret matters at all hours of the day and night. But, already, the Germans were listening.

On the coast of occupied Holland, the German Post Office had set up a listening post to tap the radio-telephone link between England and America. They had even perfected a descrambling device. To their utter amazement, when they tuned in, they discovered that one of the men they were listening to was Churchill himself. From 1942 onwards, the calls from Churchill's private number—Whitehall 4433—were regularly monitored, and written reports were sent direct to Hitler. If the date of D-Day were ever to be discovered, the leak would probably come from here. But it might also come from the BBC.

Throughout the war, resistance in France was organised by the Special Operations Executive in London—the same SOE that had produced the fiasco in Holland. But in France it was more successful, and SOE planned a massive sabotage operation behind the German lines to coincide with D-Day. One way in which SOE kept in touch with its agents in France was through the personal messages sent through the French service of the BBC. From a dark basement studio in Bush House, off the Strand, came the voice of the announcer: 'Ici Londres. Ici Londres. This is London. The French speaking to the French. First of all, here are some personal messages. "Leonidas was brave." "The Candles lit up our forefathers." "You can go to the cinema without any danger." ' Secretly listening in occupied France were the British agents like 'Annette'.

> In 1944, S.O.E. brought out a very compact receiver and I would lie in bed with my set under the covers so that no-one could hear anything. Broadcasts were at certain hours and we were given a transmission time-table. It was so small, about the size of a postage stamp, that we were given magnifying glasses to read it.

Yvonne Cormeau, 'Annette', had been parachuted into south-west France in 1943. As radio operator for the underground, she had both to send messages to London and to receive them. The personal message was, in both cases, her life line.

The personal message is not a code in the usual sense, though it does the same kind of job. It is a phrase, like 'Leonidas was brave', which is quite meaningless except to the sender and the receiver. They are the only people who know that it really means, say, that a parachute drop will take place on Wednesday at 20.00 hours.

Regular contact between SOE and its agents was by normal coded transmission sent over short-wave radio. But these transmissions were often jammed and the codes broken. For the quick transmission of vital information the personal message provided the answer. It could be broadcast over the public radio system and, whilst remaining absolutely secure, could be sure of reaching its destination. The personal messages were usually selected by the agent himself.

> We could choose any old thing as a personal message. One day, for instance, as I was encoding and asking S.O.E. for supplies, I noticed that some roses I had on the table had started to fade and the red one was losing its petals. So I chose as my personal message 'The Red Rose is Faded'. I wrote it down, encoded it and radioed it to London. When some days later, 'The Red Rose

is Faded' came through on the 9 o'clock news, it was the signal to me that the supplies I'd requested would be dropped that night. A little group, called a Reception Committee, then went out to the field to show the pilot and the crew where they were to drop their load. When the chutes opened and the containers dropped they were hauled away on carts as they were very heavy and hidden before daylight, away from the Germans.

The personal messages, as well as providing warning signals, also provided the anonymous agent with a means of establishing his identity. Agent César, operating alone in eastern France, was desperate for money. He asked for a loan from a known British sympathiser, Monsieur Peugeot, the car manufacturer. But Peugeot suspected it was a German trap and wanted proof that 'César' was really a British agent.

I asked him to make up some short message and offered to have it broadcast over the French service of the BBC. Peugeot's factory was in the Doub valley and he chose the message 'The Doub Valley is beautiful in summer'. I radioed the message to SOE and it was duly broadcast by the BBC. Peugeot was convinced and, really, it was an ideal way to establish confidence. I mean, I couldn't carry around a letter from Montgomery, or George VIth saying I was an accredited agent, could I? And the personal message was an absolutely secure way of saying I was genuine.

Winning Peugeot's confidence was to pay handsome dividends. The car factory was making tank parts for the Germans and was a prime target for the RAF. But they failed to put it out of action. César, on the spot and on the ground, suggested to Peugeot that the place be sabotaged. Peugeot gave permission and César went into action.

The factory was guarded by the Germans but a person in overalls went through easily. Peugeot put me in touch with one of his top foremen and I wandered round the place looking at things. I didn't know very much about sabotage but I had got quite a lot of explosives in store from droppings by the RAF and in November we had our first great blow up. The Germans were absolutely astonished. Nothing like it had happened before and we stopped production for a week. From then on they were blowing up machines right till the end of the war.

This extraordinary effort by the agents of SOE was, of course, directed to one end—the liberation of France. By the spring of 1944 it was only a matter of weeks before the planned invasion. On the opposite side of the Channel, the Germans, under Rommel, spiked the beaches with stakes and buried five million land mines. But Rommel was worried. Without detailed information about Allied intentions he was forced to spread his men along the entire length of the Channel coast, which ensured that 60 per cent of his defence was bound to be in the wrong place when invasion came. If only he could find out where the landings were to take place, he could concentrate his forces and repel the attack. The German listening posts strained for the information that could make all the difference between victory and defeat.

Then, in early March 1944, they thought they had hit the jackpot. Churchill on the phone to Roosevelt. The conversation, according to the report sent to Himmler, lasted nearly five minutes and 'disclosed a crescendo of military activity in Britain, thereby corroborating the many reports of impending invasion.' But Churchill had not mentioned the date. The Germans, for the time being, remained in the dark.

By the end of May, 'Operation Overlord' was ready. On 2 June the final complement of amphibious craft was driven to the coast. On 3 June the final troops embarked. All that was needed now was good flying weather and the right tides. But on 4 June heavy cloud postponed operations for twenty-four hours.

In France the agents had already received their orders. Each group had been given two individual personal messages. Although, when the day came, hundreds would be broadcast, they were not to act until they heard their own. The first would mean 'Stand by, invasion imminent'; the second, 'Invasion begun—start sabotage operations'.

But already there was danger. César:

> You might have ten people, even more, who would need to know the personal message—and if they started talking, and they told their wives or their girl friends, it could very well get out to the Germans.

Two of the messages had already been passed on—probably by an informer. One was 'Les sanglots longues des violons de l'automne' and the other 'blessent mon coeur d'une langueur monotone'. If the BBC broadcast them, the Germans were pretty sure they knew what was coming.

In the Baker Street HQ of SOE, the countdown to 'Operation Overlord' had already begun. The D-Day warning messages were placed in a sealed envelope and sent by woman despatch rider to the BBC. As the news-reader began the long list of messages, the whole of the French underground was tuned in. Annette:

> We were waiting. Taking it in turns. The message for our little group was simply 'He's got a weird voice'. When I heard it I was in the loft of a barn. I didn't even bother to go down the ladder. I jumped down to tell everybody about it because this was really the culminating moment of our whole mission.
>
> When it was dark, all the men went round and got their material out of the hiding places, cleaned the weapons, struck the ammunition and were ready to move the next day.

As well as the whole French underground, the Germans were

listening too. Over the loudspeaker came the words 'Les sang-lots longues des violons de l'automne'. The message was rushed round to Rommel at the OKV headquarters. He studied it, decided it meant invasion in two weeks' time, and went home to Germany to celebrate his wife's birthday. Annette:

> Then there was a second message which came over which was the one to tell us to move. This meant our guerilla men had to go out—damage the rail centres, blow up roads, demolish bridges, pylons, anything which would prevent the enemy in the Pyrenees, where we were, from going up towards the Normandy district.

The German listening stations, unaware of Rommel's decision, strained for the second message. It came within twenty-four hours: 'blessent mon coeur d'une langueur monotone'. It was probably the most important message the Germans had intercepted throughout the whole of the war.

The German commander-in-charge, in Rommel's absence, thought the message was a phoney. He delayed sending any warning to the German armies until a mere three hours before the first Allied troops dropped in Normandy. By then, it was too late. And the German Seventh Army, which was to receive the brunt of the attack, was somehow never told at all. The Germans had spent four years trying to discover the date of the D-Day landings. When the information came, they failed to recognise it. And they paid the price.

But all was not yet lost. The Allies had only a toe-hold in Normandy and the Germans had reserves all over France. These reserves were immediately summoned to the beaches. One of them was the crack Panzer Division stationed in the Pyrenees, and it was the job of Annette's group to prevent it from getting there.

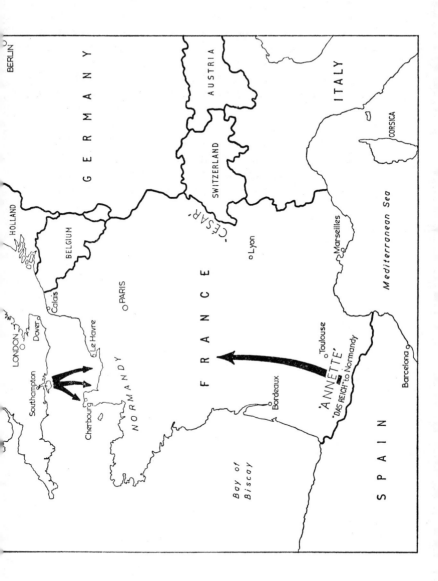

The German Division 'Das Reich' started to go north but when we heard they were moving, the boss immediately made preparations for us to block them in the usual way. They didn't get very far—a bridge was up here, a railway line cut there. So they had to go a long way round which delayed them considerably and gave our men in Normandy more time to get a proper foothold.

It is now known that if the German Panzers from the Pyrenees had reached Normandy in time, they would probably have saved the entire German situation. But they did not. And the personal messages sent to Annette probably saved the day.

# 16  *Message to Moscow*

After the Allied victory in World War II, the Iron Curtain clanged down across Europe. With the onset of the Cold War, codes and ciphers took on a new lease of life. The expertise developed by the intelligence bureaux in war time was put to good use. However the chief users were no longer the military, but the spies, and they operated on both sides of the Curtain.

Helen and Peter Kroger, gaoled in Britain in 1961, were the most capable spies ever caught in this country. They were spying for Russia and the object of their attentions was the Admiralty's Underwater Weapons Research Establishment at Portland in Dorset. It was the Western Alliance Headquarters for research into submarines and underwater devices.

The Portland spy ring consisted of two Britons, Ethel Gee and Harry Houghton, who worked at Portland and stole the secrets; the Krogers themselves, whose real name was Cohen and who had a long history as professional spies in the United States; and the ring master—Gordon Lonsdale, who passed himself off as a Canadian but who was probably an intelligence officer in the Russian navy. In many respects the Portland ring was a direct development of the Lucy ring. The spy techniques that the Krogers used were updated and improved versions of the extremely effective ones already used by the Russians twelve years before in Switzerland.

The ring's communications experts were the Krogers and it was their job to pass on the secrets to Moscow. To do it successfully, they needed to establish themselves in the community as an absolutely ordinary couple. They bought a bungalow in Ruislip—with money from Moscow—and invited their neighbours in for drinks. Mr Kroger set himself up in the second-hand book business, and was a familiar and respected figure at book auctions. He kept his books at home and, to protect them, fitted good locks on all the doors and anti-theft devices on all the windows. They kept out all potential book thieves, and, without raising suspicion, kept everybody else out as well.

The book-dealing cover also gave Kroger complete freedom of movement. No one was surprised if he did a lot of his work at home. No one was suspicious if, in the course of business, he had to travel abroad—even to the Book Fairs behind the Iron Curtain. The Kroger camouflage was brilliant, and could hardly have been bettered; it was another member of the ring, Lonsdale, who gave the Krogers away. Lonsdale, instead of using cut-outs, visited the Krogers direct. Already under police suspicion, he was regularly trailed to Ruislip and gave the police the information they wanted. On a wet Saturday evening, 7 January 1961, the late Superintendent Smith of Scotland Yard arrived at Cranley Drive.

There wasn't a single soul about. No-one at all. No curtains drawn aside. No aspidistra faces or anything like that at the windows. I knocked at the door shortly after 6.30 p.m. I knew Lonsdale arrived somewhere between 6.30 and a quarter to seven. It's doubtful whether we'd have succeeded in getting in with a jemmy as there was a Yale lock and a mortice lock on the door and two big bolts as well. I waited and the bolts were drawn back and the keys turned and then Kroger himself appeared. I told him we were police officers and I'd like to see him. I had one foot in the door, of course, just in case, but he invited us in and led the way into the lounge. Mrs. Kroger wasn't there and I wanted to see her too. I waited a few moments, and I could hear someone else in the house, and after a second or two she came into the room. I said to them; 'I'm a superintendent of the Special Branch and I've come to see you as we've got reason to believe you've been committing infringements of the Official Secrets Act.'

The Krogers were arrested and were to be taken to Hayes police station to be formally charged. They went upstairs to get their clothes.

Mrs. Kroger went into the bedroom accompanied by a police woman. As she entered, she gently closed the door and, after a second or two, I pushed it open just in time to hear her ask the police woman to give her something. As the officer turned her back, I saw Mrs. Kroger, and she had her overcoat on by this time, bend down and take up something from a chair. She then faced me and came out into the hall and said, 'Oh Superintendent, as we appear to be going away for a long time, have you any objection if I stoke the boiler fire?' And I said, 'Certainly not. But first of all would you let me see what you've got in your handbag?' She wouldn't. So I took the bag and opened it up. Inside was a small white envelope and inside the envelope a single sheet of paper bearing a block of typed numbers.

On closer inspection, this proved to be a cipher message ready for despatch to Moscow, and the device used for encipherment was the 'one-time pad'.

The one-time pad is unbreakable, a development of the cipher used by the Lucy ring. Lucy enciphered their messages by a once-only reference to numbers in a book of statistics. With the one-time pad, the difference is that the numbers are already provided by Intelligence HQ—in this case, Moscow. As it is no longer necessary to search through an ordinary book, the method is quicker, eliminates mistakes and does away with the need for a key-group. Moreover, the one-time pad itself, about an inch square, is easier to conceal and to carry about than a large statistics book. The pad looks like a small book of raffle tickets—as many as 200 tickets in all. On each ticket is, not one number, but maybe a hundred set out in groups of four (Fig. 33). These are the groups used to encipher the message, and each page is used only once. When a page is finished, it is torn off and the next message is enciphered by a different set of codenumber groups on the second ticket—and so on. Because the number groups are never the same, no two plain-text letters can be enciphered the same, so the cipher is unbreakable.

This is how the pad works. A report is to be made to Moscow beginning, say, 'Polaris at Portland'. The first step is to

| | | | | |
|---|---|---|---|---|
| 3989 | 2098 | 7291 | 6654 | 2017 |
| 8635 | 8100 | 5629 | 7611 | 8590 |
| 2245 | 9463 | 2105 | 4957 | 0011 |
| 8842 | 5937 | 6891 | 3421 | 7072 |
| 6543 | 1235 | 9964 | 1849 | 0386 |
| 4638 | 9461 | 8408 | 6674 | 3777 |
| 3300 | 4884 | 1884 | 9327 | 8639 |
| 5692 | 9375 | 7003 | 2947 | 3655 |
| 0742 | 4598 | 7364 | 7638 | 1770 |
| 9597 | 5287 | 1392 | 9672 | 0617 |
| 3561 | 8546 | 2081 | 4598 | 8472 |
| 9533 | 8563 | 8645 | 6842 | 0625 |
| 3581 | 8549 | 9251 | 7643 | 9799 |
| 1020 | 7729 | 5562 | 9573 | 3626 |

*Page of one-time pad*

Fig. 33

split the words into separate letters and number them according to a prearranged plan. The simplest is to number A to Z as 1 to 26.

Then step two is to read the numbers on the top sheet of the one-time pad from left to right and add them to the existing numbers. It ends up like this (using carrying addition):

| P | O | L | A | R | I | S | A | T |
|---|---|---|---|---|---|---|---|---|
| 16 | 15 | 12 | 1 | 18 | 9 | 19 | 1 | 20 |
| 3989 | 2098 | 7291 | 6654 | 2017 | 8365 | 8100 | 5629 | 7611 |
| 4005 | 2113 | 7303 | 6655 | 2035 | 8374 | 8119 | 5630 | 7631 |

| P | O | R | T | L | A | N | D |
|---|---|---|---|---|---|---|---|
| 16 | 15 | 18 | 20 | 12 | 1 | 14 | 4 |
| 8590 | 2245 | 9463 | 2105 | 4957 | 0011 | 8842 | 5937 |
| 8606 | 2260 | 9481 | 2125 | 4969 | 0012 | 8856 | 5941 |

The ingeniousness of the pad is obvious. Both 'Polaris' and 'Portland' start with the same letter. In one case P is enciphered 4005 and in the second 8606. O is enciphered 2113 and 2260. A, repeated three times, is enciphered 6655, 5630 and 0012. So a normal frequency count cannot work, as there are no repetitions to count.

For all its impregnability, there are some problems. One is that if it is a long message, it takes time to encipher and the spy needs to remain undisturbed. The Krogers were able to lock themselves in. Another is that only two copies of a pad are allowed to exist—the spy's and the one in headquarters. It is essential for the decoder in HQ to use the same page of the pad as the spy. Once they are no longer synchronised, the messages become unintelligible. Finally, although the pad is small it can still be detected. Moscow therefore printed its pads on cellulose nitrate film, which burns vigorously. If a spy is caught, the pad can be destroyed very quickly. (Mrs Kroger, remember, made the not-so-innocent request to stoke the boiler.)

With the Krogers out of the way, Superintendent Smith was free to search the house for further incriminating evidence. It involved digging up floors, stripping furniture and meticulously examining personal effects.

In the lounge, in the waste paper basket was a piece of flex forty-seven and a half feet long. What on earth was it used for? Was it an aerial? If it was, then where was the transmitter? We searched for several days and in the end we used mine detectors and came to the kitchen. We moved all the heavy furniture and right above the big refrigerator was a trap door. We opened it up to reveal a hole about three and a half feet deep. It seemed to be filled with rubble. We began to tap around down there with hammers and discovered a small crack in the concrete. It was very difficult to lever up because the slab of concrete was four inches thick, but underneath, covered with a piece of wood and wrapped in cellophane, was what we'd been looking for. The transmitter. When we examined it we got to calling it the United Nations transmitter because it was made up from parts from almost every country in the world—except Russia.

True to form, just as they always enciphered in English, the Russians made sure their equipment could never be associated with the Soviet Union. The transmitter was much bigger than the ones the Dutchmen, for example, had had to cart around in war time. Bigger, even, than the ones the Lucy ring used, and more sophisticated, as the chances of its being discovered *in situ* were minimal. The only danger came from detection-finders, from the police tracking the transmitter down whilst it was actually on air. It was in this way that the police had caught both 'Edward, and 'Jim' in Switzerland.

The Russians, learning from those past mistakes, took steps

to make detection almost impossible. The major precaution was the choice of the bungalow's position. It was situated close to three local aerodromes: Heathrow itself, the RAF at Northolt and the Americans in South Ruislip. The Russian idea was that any radio traffic sent by the Krogers to Moscow would easily get lost in the regular chatter between aeroplanes and their control towers, and transmission frequencies were deliberately chosen to be as close to airport frequencies as possible.

To achieve the ultimate in message safety, the Krogers used a high-speed keying device. It looks like a cross between a tape-recorder and a typewriter. The morse code dots and dashes are punched onto a ribbon. The ribbon is rewound and then played at ten, or even twenty, times the normal transmission speed. To make the message intelligible in Moscow, HQ records the message as it comes in at high speed and then merely slows the tape down. But during the danger time of transmission, the message sounds merely like a high-pitched buzz that is more likely to be mistaken for atmospheric interference than recognised as somebody broadcasting. Nevertheless, during the Krogers' time at Ruislip, a local radio ham complained to the Post Office of unusually strong radio interference in the neighbourhood. But no investigation was made. It is interesting to speculate how many secrets would have been saved from the Russians if action had been taken!

In the past, spies have made use of false heels, cavities in teeth, and secret pockets, and one ancient Persian, to keep his secrets safe, even used his slave's head. He shaved the hair, tattooed a message on the bald skin, and, when the hair had grown, sent the slave and the message to a contact in Greece. To read the message the Greek merely cut the slave's hair. Two thousand years later the Krogers were more sophisticated. They maintained the tradition but brought it up to date, as Superintendent Smith discovered.

In the bedroom we found a very nice whisky flask full of whisky beside the bed and in the lounge we found what appeared to be a very nice Ronson lighter. After X-raying and much manipulation we found that both objects contained secret cavities. In the flask was iron oxide powder used to help them read the symbols of incoming messages recorded on magnetic tape. And in the lighter were sets of signal plans and some one-time code pads.

The signal plans were sent from Moscow to tell the Krogers at what time to make their transmissions, and the pads were regular replacements for those already used up. Significantly, the cellulose nitrate pads were stored in a working cigarette lighter so that the Krogers always had a ready flame handy if the pads needed to be destroyed in a hurry. The lighter and the flask looked exactly like the real thing. In fact they were triumphs of Russian workmanship, specially manufactured for export, to the spy rings in the West.

In the bathroom, like everywhere else heavily reinforced with locks, we found three talc powder tins. We found that if we took the top off the tin completely, there were two secret cavities inside. On one side were stored some small negatives with more signal plans on, and in the other, a tiny magnifying glass. We also found some boards that fitted over the windows.

The bathroom must have been used as a dark room. But as Mr Kroger was not known for his amateur photography, what else might he be up to?

Up in the loft we found large quantities of photographic material and several cameras. And in the study downstairs, in the family Bible, was a piece of paper about four inches by five. It seemed like photographic paper.

Things were beginning to fall into place. What Kroger was really doing was making microdots. The tiny magnifying glass was a microdot reader; the cameras were used for photographing messages and the photographic paper for making the dots themselves.

The microdot was a method of secret communication that could be used as an addition to the one-time pad or as an alternative if the pad, for some reason, failed. The first ever microdot was picked up late in the last war, on a letter intercepted at the Bermuda censorship station. Since then, the device became more widely used until, with the code, it became one of the chief weapons in the armoury of the peacetime spy.

The aim is to reduce a page of a document, perhaps a foot square and containing 350 words, to a dot no larger than a full stop. This is done by photographing through what is effectively the reverse end of a telescope. Instead of magnifying the object and appearing to bring it closer, it distances it and makes it smaller. The more powerful the lens the smaller the image is, and it is this tiny image that is photographed and appears on the negative as no more than a dot. It is cut out of the negative with a hypodermic needle that has been cut off short to produce a tiny punch. Stuck on a letter or postcard, the dot looks just like a piece of punctuation.

For security intelligence trying to track them down in the ordinary mail, it is worse than looking for the proverbial needle in a haystack. And if the spy wants to be really clever the microdots, normally black, can be bleached pale yellow so as to be invisible on ordinary writing paper. But, for the recipient, they are simple to read. Slipped into the base of the microdot reader, like the one the Krogers had, they are magnified a thousand times. For Peter Kroger, microdots were ideal. As a dealer in old books by post, he could send his microdots to any place in the world whenever he needed to.

The Krogers were perfectionists, master spies. Their techniques of enciphering and transmission; their mastery of the microdot; their brilliant security; their cover activities; their hiding places, even the locks on the front door, can barely be faulted. If Gordon Lonsdale had not made regular visits to their home, but had learnt from the experience of the Lucy ring and communicated through a cut-out, the Krogers might never have been caught. Even though they were, the friendly neighbours, Peter and Helen, did more to destroy the security and naval effectiveness of the Western Allies than any other couple in history.

# 17 *What Next?*

The methods used by the Krogers are still used today. In London's Central Criminal Court in 1971 two men were charged with 'conspiracy to communicate information for a purpose prejudicial to the state'. In evidence, it was reported how police officers had discovered 'what appeared to be two perfectly ordinary torch batteries but when the tops were unscrewed there was revealed a hollowed-out cavity in each containing film and a signal plan'. The evidence continued: 'In a cash box in the bedroom was what appeared to be an ordinary dark green lead pencil. When the top was unscrewed a cavity was disclosed, a convenient hiding place for microfilm and coded messages'. It was like the Kroger case all over again—only ten years later.

Secret intelligence is a game played by all nations. And there are rules. Be discreet and don't get caught. Blatant spying leads to political and diplomatic wrangling embarrassing to both sides. As long as it is kept in bounds, countries prefer to turn a blind eye to enemy intelligence. And there are very sound reasons for doing so. It is much more secure for counter-espionage to let a spy continue working and know what he is doing than to expel him and have to start from scratch with his replacement. It is a question of better the spy you know than the one you have not located.

But occasionally things get out of hand. When, in 1971, a Russian official was caught red-handed leaving coded messages in a tin can on Hampstead Heath (he was using the excellent cut-out technique rather too blatantly), the British felt he had breeched the bounds of hospitality. Over one hundred Russians, including diplomats, trade officials and airline employees, were expelled from Britain for alleged spying. Moscow was annoyed, less because they had been found out, than because the British had made an embarrassing fuss. The Russians retaliated and the British Embassy in Moscow was suddenly several employees short. But the Russians, like everyone else, prefer to be discreet. And the American tourists and protesting British businessmen suddenly thrust out of the Soviet Union are rarely the innocent victims that the western press makes out.

There are probably more spies in the world today than ever before. It is a growth industry, and the biggest growth area is in industrial espionage. As commercial success now largely depends on developing new projects ahead of competitors, spying on rival companies' research projects has become big business. There was a recent case of secrets allegedly stolen from Kodak. It had the classic ingredients of mysterious packages and coded messages left behind the lavatory cistern of trans-continental trains. More recent still is the case of the Concorde—if there really is a case. Many people have asked why two epoch-making aircraft like the Anglo-French Concorde and the Russian rival, nicknamed Concordski, look almost identical. Is it coincidence or is it something else? We shall probably never know, but what is certain is that industrial espionage on an international scale will continue to increase.

As the areas of espionage interest have changed, so have the spying techniques. The human element is gradually being replaced by advanced technology. High-flying spy-planes equipped with cameras that can photograph the contents of a document through the walls of a room and from several miles up can prove more effective than a human being. Methods of transmission have changed, too. Morse code may soon be replaced by light signals, invisible to the naked eye, which can be bounced off the moon. But, despite all this, there is still a secure place for cryptology.

The traditional pencil-and-paper code techniques have, over the last fifty years, become slicker, more sophisticated. But the basic principles have remained the same. And so have the jobs they are intended to do. Behind the respectable diplomatic façades of the embassies of London's St John's Wood or Washington's Constitution Avenue, or of any big city in the world, are an army of code-clerks all busy encoding and enciphering and transmitting military and diplomatic secrets to their own countries. And in respectable suburbia, or city parks, even on the high seas, spies and intelligence agents are doing the same thing. For as long as there are people with secrets to hide, there will be a use for codes and ciphers to hide them—at least in the foreseeable future.

# Sources and Bibliography

Because of the secrecy that surrounds the subject, few books have been published on the history of cryptography. I can recommend three: *Secret and Urgent*, by Fletcher Pratt (New York, 1942); *Elementary Cryptanalysis*, by Helen Gaines (London, 1940); and the book I have drawn on most heavily, David Khan's *The Codebreakers* (London, 1966).

A great deal of my information has come first hand from the cryptographers and secret agents themselves. I list these interviews along with books, other than the above, which have supplied background material for specific chapters. The place of publication is London unless otherwise stated, and the sequence of sources follows that in the text.

J. H. Pollen, *Mary Queen of Scots and the Babington Plot* (Edinburgh, 1922)

A. G. Smith, *The Babington Plot* (1936)

Barbara Tuckman, *The Zimmerman Telegram* (New York, 1958)

Admiral Sir William James, *The Eyes of the Navy, a study of Admiral Hall* (1956)

Professor Bruford, interview, 22 May 1970

Professor Willoughby, interview, 19 May 1970

Miss May Jenkin, interview, 14 July 1970

Admiral Sir William James, interview, 8 April 1970

Professor Hermann Stutzel (German cryptanalyst, World War I), interview, June 1970

General Ludendorff. *My War Memories 1914-1918* (1919)

Colonel Fritz Nabel, interview, 6 August 1971

Colonel Georges Painvin, interview, 8 July 1971

Captain J. Rives Childs (Head of US Army Cipher Bureau, who worked on ADFGX), interview, 6 July 1971

M. F. Willoughby, *Rum War at Sea* (Washington, 1964)

Irving Brown (US Customs official during Prohibition), interview, 31 August 1971

Mrs Elizabeth Friedman, interview, 31 August 1971

Lt Alfred Powell, interview, 31 August 1971

E. L. Bentley, *Complete Phrase Code Book* (6th ed, 1920)

Reports in *The Times, Morning Post,* and *Daily Telegraph,* 20 March 1929

Reports of court case in above papers, 28 December 1934.

Mrs Nadya Letteney, interview, 16 June 1970

H. Montgomery Hyde (security officer at Bermuda), interview, 26 June 1970

'Cabbage', interview, 20 May 1970

H. J. Giskes, *London Calling North Pole* (1953)

Major Herman Giskes, interview, 23 May 1970

Pieter Dourlein, *Inside North Pole* (1953)

Pieter Dourlein, interview, 1 June 1970

Herbert Yardley, *The American Black Chamber* (Indianapolis, 1931)

Walter Lord, *Day of Infamy* (New York, 1957)

George Margenstern, *Pearl Harbor* (New York, 1947)

Mrs Elizabeth Friedman, interview, 8 June 1970

Captain J. Rochefort, interview, 22 June 1970

Admiral A. H. McCollum, interview, 18 June 1970

Commander Mitsuo Fuchida, interview, 1 July 1970

General B. F. Fellers, interview, 15 May 1970

Cesare Amé, *Guerra Segreta in Italia 1940-1943* (Rome, 1954)

General Cesare Amé, interview, 21 May 1970

Dr Herbert Schaedel, interview, May 1970

General Siegfried Westphal, interview, 28 May 1970

W. S. Churchill, *History of the Second World War*, vols 3–5 (1950-2)

## Sources and Bibliography

Giorgio Pillon, *Spie per l'Italia* (Rome, 1968)

Commander Gordon Bridson, interview, July 1970

Captain Alva Lasswell, interview, 22 June 1970

Captain John Mitchell, interview, 22 June 1970

Captain Thomas Lanphier, interview, 16 June 1970

Drago Arsenijevic, *Geneve appelle Moscou* (Paris, 1969)

Sando Rado, *Dora Jelenti* (Budapest, 1971)

Sando Rado, telephone conversation, September 1971

Otto Punter, *Guerre Secrète en Pays Neutre* (Lausanne, 1967)

Otto Punter, interview, 25 August 1971.

Edmund Hammel, interview, 24 August 1971

Alexander Foote, *Handbook for Spies* (1949)

Mayer von Baldegg (Swiss secret service), interview, 23 August 1971

Marcel Payot (Swiss Army cryptanalyst), interview, 25 August 1971

Rudolph Knecht (Swiss police chief who arrested Foote), interview, 22 August 1971

M. R. D. Foot, *S.O.E. in France* (1966)

J. C. Masterman, *Double Cross System* (Yale University Press, 1972)

Maurice Belfer (BBC French Service announcer), interview, 11 August 1971

Mrs Yvonne Cormeau, interview, 11 August 1971

Professor Harry Ree, interview, 13 August 1971

Cornelius Ryan, *The Longest Day* (New York, 1959)

David Howarth, *D-Day: the Sixth of June 1944* (New York, 1959)

Superintendent Smith, interview, 21 May 1970

Superintendent Smith, 'Soviet Spy Ring' (1962)

Report in *The Times*, 14 March 1961

# Index

*Index*

# G

# H

# I

# J

# N

Nabel, Colonel Fritz, 63–5
Nulls, 17, 40, 99, 105, 134

# O

Operation Fortitude, 153; North Pole, 97–108, 152; Overlord, 152–62

# P

Painvin, Georges, 67–71
Paulus, Marshal Von, 147, 150
Pearl Harbor, 109, 116–22, 132
Peugot, M, 157
Phelippes, Thomas, 31–2
Philip II, King of Spain, 30, 33
Porta, Giovanni Battista, 24–7
Portland, Underwater Weapons Research Establishment, 163
Powell, Lt, 78
Prohibition in USA, 72, 74, 81
Punter, Otto, 141, 151

# R

Rado, Sandor, 141, 148, 151
Rennenkampf, General, 61–2
Repetition as an aid to decoding, 27, 43–5, 167
Rochefort, Captain Joseph, 116–17
Roessler, Rudolf, 143, 151
Rommel, Field Marshal, 123, 127, 130–1, 158, 160
Room, 40, 47–60, 62, 110
Roosevelt, President F. D., 109, 155, 158